Oxford Heritage Wa

Oxford Heritage Walks
On foot from the High to Trill Mill

Malcolm Graham
Illustrated by Edith Gollnast
Cartography by Alun Jones

OXFORD
PRESERVATION
TRUST

Oxford Preservation Trust

www.oxfordpreservation.org.uk

First published in Great Britain 2020

Illustrations produced by Edith Gollnast
Map produced by Alun Jones
Frontispiece, and illustrations nos 29, 30 & 34 by Laura Potter
Designed by Nick Clarke

Copyright © Oxford Preservation Trust 2020

All rights reserved. No parts of this work may be reproduced, stored in a retrieval system, or transmitted, in any form or by an means, electronic, mechanical, photocopying, recording or otherwise, without the prior permission of the publishers.

A catalogue of this book is available from the British Library
978–0–9576797–7–1

Printed and bound at Holywell Press, Oxford

ALSO IN THE OXFORD HERITAGE WALKS SERIES

Book 1: On foot from Oxford Castle to St Giles'

Book 2: On foot from Broad Street

Book 3: On foot from Catte Street to Parson's Pleasure

Book 4: On foot from Paradise Street to Sheepwash

Book 5: On foot from Carfax to Turn Again

Contents

About Oxford Preservation Trust — page 7

Table of Illustrations — page 9

Foreword — page 11

WALKS

1 **Carfax to Alfred Street** — page 17

2 **Alfred Street to Oriel Street** — page 23

3 **Oriel Street to Merton Street** — page 29

4 **Merton Street to Magdalen Bridge** — page 39

5 **Eastgate Hotel to Merton College** — page 45

6 **Magpie Lane to Oriel Square** — page 55

7 **Bear Lane to Blue Lamp Alley** — page 63

8 **Botanic Garden to Rose Lane** — page 71

9 **Christ Church Meadow** — page 79

10 **Folly Bridge to Speedwell Street** — page 91

11 **Speedwell Street to Christ Church** — page 101

12 **Pembroke Street to Town Hall** — page 109

About Oxford Preservation Trust

Oxford Preservation Trust is a well-established and forward-thinking charity which owns, restores and cares for land and buildings in the City, its setting and its views. A significant part of our work is in providing public open access, not least through the success of our project Oxford Open Doors, and in sharing and encouraging an interest in the City and its history.

Throughout its history Oxford has changed and expanded, and throughout the life of the Trust this has been accepted and embraced. Our work is to guide that change and not to stop it. Sir Michael Sadler, founder Trustee, states in the Trust's First Annual Report in 1927:

"Oxford is growing. Its growth may be guided but should not be grudged. The work of the Trust is not to hamper Oxford but to help it. The beauty of Oxford is one of the treasures of the world."

Sir Michael Sadler, founder Trustee, OPT Annual Report (1927)

This guide records some of the changes that have happened within our beautiful city. It fills in some of the gaps, and records some of the lost buildings and memories, building up a picture and helping to make sense of Oxford's rich history, so that it can be better appreciated and enjoyed, now and in the future. These series of books are a reminder of the contribution more modest buildings and features make to our enjoyment of the streetscapes and skyline and of their importance to the city.

We are delighted that these Heritage Walks will enable a new audience to get to know and appreciate more about Oxford. Debbie Dance, Director, 2019

Oxford Preservation Trust thanks the Greening Lamborn Trust, CPRE Oxfordshire Buildings Preservation Trust, the Barnsbury Charitable Trust, Mrs Margaret Leighfield and the William Delafield Charitable Trust for their generous donations to this project. We record our gratitude to Alun Jones, who died in 2018, leaving behind his characterful maps for us to use, and to John Ashdown for his architectural and historical advice.

The Greening Lamborn Trust's objective is to promote public interest in the history, architecture, old photographs and heraldry of Oxford and its neighbourhood by supporting publications and other media that create access to them.

Table of Illustrations

1 Carfax to Alfred Street
1. Mastiff and clock, Payne & Son, 131 High Street
2. Angels and musical instruments, All Bar One, 124 High Street

2 Alfred Street to Oriel Street
3. Tackley's Inn, rear elevation from an old drawing, 106–7 High Street

3 Oriel Street to Merton Street
4. Shelley Memorial dome in street scene, University College
5. Queen Anne statue, University College gate-tower
6. Dragon boot-scrapers outside Examination Schools
7. Carved frieze detail, squirrels, foliage and date-stone, Ruskin School of Art

4 Merton Street to Magdalen Bridge
8. Cartouche on Eastgate Hotel

5 Eastgate Hotel to Merton College
9. Red rose on Merton Street screen to Examination Schools
10. View north along Logic Lane
11. St John the Baptist sculpture, Merton College gateway
12. Glimpse of Merton Real Tennis Court, Merton Street
13. Former Merton College stables, 4a Merton Street

6 Magpie Lane to Oriel Square
14. St John's parish boundary stone, Magpie Lane
15. 4 Oriel Street

7 Bear Lane to Blue Lamp Alley
16. Carved head, Shepherd & Woodward shopfront, 109 High Street
17. St Columba's Church, Alfred Street
18. Former Oxford Gymnasium, Alfred Street
19. Chiang-Mai Restaurant, 130a High Street
20. 15th century stone panelling, bar of Chequers Inn, 131a High Street

8 Botanic Garden to Rose Lane
21. Sculpted head of goddess Isis, Magdalen Bridge
22. Bacchic Vase, Botanic Garden

9 Christ Church Meadow
23. Meadow Cottages, Rose Lane
24. Jubilee Bridge over river Cherwell
25. Eastern end of Shire Lake ditch
26. Bastion and city wall along Dead Man's Walk
27. Christ Church Masters' Garden and Cathedral
28. Longhorn cattle in Christ Church Meadow (*not shown on map*)
29. College barge, formerly moored at Dean's Ham (*not shown on map*)
30. Grandpont House

10 Folly Bridge to Speedwell Street
31. Preserved crane from Salter's Yard, Head of the River pub
32. Iron railings, Head of the River pub
33. Friar Bacon's Study from a sketch by John Malchair, 1765
34. Caudwell's Castle, 5 Folly Bridge
35. Crown Court, former Morris Garages, and bas relief of Lord Nuffield, St Aldate's

11 Speedwell Street to Christ Church
36. Trill Mill Stream from stone footbridge, Christ Church Memorial Garden

12 Pembroke Street to Town Hall
37. Detail of carved frieze on the General Post Office, St Aldate's
38. Mr Therm on balcony of former gas company showroom, 117–19 St Aldate's
39. Beaver on lead rainwater pipe, Oxford Town Hall
40. City Mace Bearer (*not shown on map*)

Foreword

This book is the sixth and last in the series of Oxford Heritage Walks books covering the city centre. The series revisits and expands on the On Foot in Oxford leaflets and booklets published by Oxford City Libraries and Oxfordshire County Libraries between 1973 and 1988. These trails were written by Malcolm Graham, Local Studies Librarian for Oxford City until 1974 and for Oxfordshire from 1974. Twelve were published in all, with local artists supplying the drawings for these trails, Laura Potter for the first eight and Edith Gollnast for the others.

Like the earlier trails, this series of Oxford Heritage Walks seeks to encourage interest in the history of the city and the evolution of the built environment. They are not primarily guides to Oxford's world-famous architectural treasures, for which there are many alternative sources. Rather, they explore how each area has developed, and focus attention on the streets and buildings of local importance which add character to every corner of our city. They are a treasure-chest of information about Oxford and offer a veritable arsenal of historical evidence for defending those features which make the city a special place.

About Oxford Heritage Walks

Author

Malcolm Graham read History at Nottingham University before doing a postgraduate librarianship course in Leeds and an MA in English Local History at Leicester University. He came to Oxford in 1970 as the City's first full-time local history librarian and took on the same role for the County in 1974. Between 1991 and 2008, he was Head of Oxfordshire Studies with Oxfordshire County Council. He has published extensively on local history – his first On Foot in Oxford town trail appeared in 1973 – and he has given hundreds of talks and broadcasts over the years. He was awarded a PhD by Leicester University for a study of the development of Oxford's Victorian suburbs and he is a Fellow of the Society of Antiquaries of London. Away from local history, he enjoys walking, cycling, outdoor swimming, music and the theatre. He is married and lives in Botley.

Illustrator

Edith Gollnast studied art and design at Banbury School of Art and architectural conservation at Bristol University. For thirty five years she worked with historic buildings and areas at Oxford City Council. Edith lives in Oxford, where she enjoys creative activities, the arts and walking.

Cartographer

Alun Jones (1927-2018) was a Cartographer who created clear handwritten maps, often combining historical information and topography. His Classics degree was followed by the Diploma in Classical Archaeology at Oxford University in 1952; his fieldwork involved training in photography, Land Survey and technical drawing (using the traditional instruments of pre-digital recording). The history and practice of letters and writing, cartography, calligraphy and printing and book production were major interests while on the Staff of the Printer to the University (Oxford University Press) and then at the Alden Press, Oxford (1958-1982). Alun was later appointed Dean of the Centre for Medieval Studies, Oxford. Many of his maps were made for Oxford Preservation Trust, CPRE Oxfordshire and the Garden History Society as a service to the community. In 2001 he was elected a Fellow of the British Cartographic Society. Alun died in 2018, but will live on through his maps.

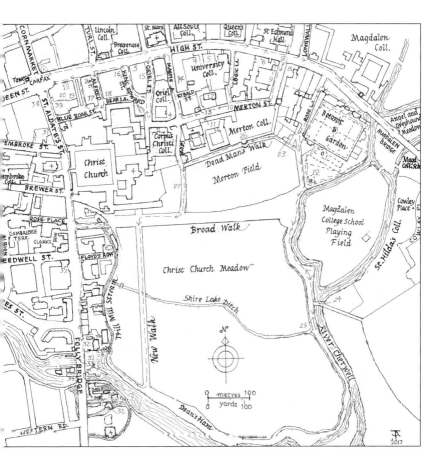

The twelve sections in this book can be combined to provide three linear walks through some of Oxford's most memorable streets and spaces. Sections 1 to 4 take you along the north side of High Street from Carfax to Magdalen Bridge. Sections 5 to 7 return you to Carfax by way of the delightful streets and lanes south of High Street. Sections 8 to 12 offer a very different but equally tempting route from Magdalen Bridge to Carfax, taking in the Botanic Garden, Christ Church Meadow and Folly Bridge.

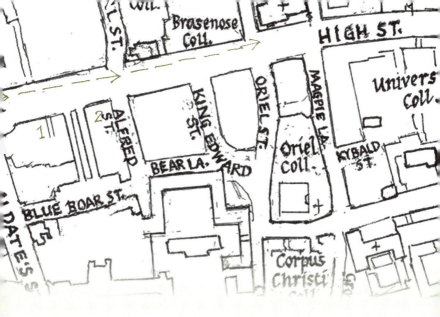

1 Carfax to Alfred Street

High Street originated in c.900 as one of the principal roads of the Saxon burh. Initially, High Street probably terminated at an east gate where St Mary the Virgin Church now stands, but Oxford's defences are thought to have been extended eastwards in the early 11th century to a point near the present Eastgate Hotel. This extension created High Street's famous curve, noted in Wordsworth's description of 'the stream-like windings of that glorious street.' Houses and churches were built on both sides, and university halls and colleges began to appear among them in the 12th century. Leonard Hutten, in the 1620s, remarked that High Street was 'the fairest and longest streete of the Citty... continued, on both sides, with Cittizens Houses all the length.' He chose to overlook All Souls College and University College, but his description is a reminder that High Street was as much a Town as a Gown thoroughfare. The street was filled with stalls on market days in medieval times and sellers of straw for thatching roofs occupied the centre of the road between All Saints' Church and the Eastgate. Pigs were sold outside All Saints' Church, now Lincoln College Library, until 1684, and butchers set up their stalls between Carfax and Turl Street on market days until the 1770s. Following the Oxford Improvement Act of 1771, these obstructions were swept away and High Street, was paved by 1779, with stone pavements and side gutters replacing a central drainage channel.

Especially at this west end of High Street, former citizens' houses are still very evident, but many of the tall, timber-framed and jettied houses that so impressed Hutten have been rebuilt, hidden behind later façades or replaced by commercial, college, or university developments. The overall result, however, has been to create what Nikolaus Pevsner described as 'one of the world's great streets.' In this walk, we shall concentrate on the buildings on the south side of High Street, best viewed from the pavement on the other side. Almost every building you will see has been listed as being of architectural and historical interest, and the few unlisted ones have at least a local significance. It also perhaps needs saying that some of today's listed structures are on the sites of buildings that we would have cherished had they survived the ravages of time.

Beginning outside Lloyd's Bank, your first view is of Marygold House (1932, Ashley & Newman) on the south-east corner of Carfax. Like its stylistic partner, Abbey House, on the opposite corner, this building was the product of a major road-widening scheme at Carfax. Nos. 139–43 High Street, the last five properties on the south side, were lost to this improvement, and part of the site was added to the street. No. 143 or Carfax House, on the corner, was unusual in the Oxford context, being a plain four storey Georgian red brick building. Brick was deeply unfashionable in contemporary Oxford, but the artist Hanslip Fletcher, sent up to Oxford by the Society for the Protection of Ancient Buildings in 1931 to record the city's threatened domestic buildings, was so upset by the imminent destruction of Carfax House that, 'I drew it at once, standing on the island, in mid-traffic and just as I had finished was informed that I should have asked permission from the Superintendent of Police.' Drapers had long occupied the premises, and, at this date, Wyatt & Sons had their drapery business here. They took the ground floor shop in the new office building, and continued trading until the end of 1953. Edinburgh Wool Mill has occupied the shop premises since the 1990s.

Nos. 141–42 High Street, adjoining Carfax House, were also demolished in 1931. Both were ancient buildings, owned by the City since the 16th century. In the 1920s, no. 142 was a Great Western Railway booking office and no. 141 a shoe shop, but the latter – a building just 12 feet wide – had been occupied by Henry Andrews, a saddler and harness maker, from 1861 to 1918. A photograph of 1909 showing saddles in Andrews' window is a reminder that countrymen and women were then still riding into Oxford to buy and sell as they had done for centuries. As part of the Carfax improvement scheme, the City set a new building line for subsequent developments in High Street, and that explains the wide pavement outside the three bay stone-fronted building, formerly Martin's Bank (1938, Wills &

Kaula) on the site of nos. 139–40. The old properties here were gabled, timber-framed buildings, clearly built as a pair. Both had become pubs during the 18th century, no. 139 the Red Lion, and no. 140 the Jolly Post Boys. The Jolly Post Boys took over no. 139 in the early 1850s and remained there until 1935 when both the name and the licence were transferred to a new pub in Florence Park.

At no. 138 High Street, we are back to a narrow pavement and the old building line. Older Oxonians will recall the bus and railway booking office here, latterly known as Carfax Travel Bureau. The present three storey building (1851) has been much altered, but retains an attractive ashlar stone façade with a pedimented first floor window and a deep eaves cornice. The next building (1884, H.J. Tollit), with its half-timbering and a gable with decorative bargeboards, looks enjoyably ancient, but it was a Victorian development on the site of the Fox Inn, a pub since 1764. Hall's Oxford Brewery had a city-centre office here until 1906, and it was Savory's tobacconist's shop from 1936 until 1994. No. 136 (1933, G.T. Gardner) is a neo-Georgian style rebuild, following the 1930s building line, and thus set well back behind the street frontage. The four storey stone façade has an oriel window on the first and second floors with a delightful carved swan at its base. The previous property on the site had been a pub, the Spread Eagle or the Split Crow in the 17th century, and was the home of Panayoty Ballachey, the University's Greek fencing master in 1772.

At no. 135, you are back to the early 18th century with a three storey stuccoed timber-framed house. The upper floors have sash windows and, above the modillioned eaves cornice, there are three gabled dormers in the slate roof. Edward Lock (1729–1813), goldsmith, jeweller and banker, and three times Mayor of Oxford, occupied these premises from 1759 before moving across the road to no. 7. Since 1915, parts of the building have been used a café, the longest-lasting one being the Town & Gown Restaurant between 1925 and 1976. No. 134 also dates back to the 18th century, but we know who built it – Richard Cox (1756–1834), a draper – and when – 1790. It is effectively a taller, updated version of no. 135, again of three storeys with sash windows and attic dormers but built of ashlar stone. Cox later went into banking and was Mayor of Oxford three times, but he fled to France as a bankrupt facing corruption charges in 1833, and he died there. The upstairs part of the building became the Market Vaults Hotel by 1889, and the manager during the 1920s was Alfred Shrubb (d.1964), a former world-champion athlete who was the University's first professional athletics coach. White's Bar occupied these premises from 1936, and was a popular drinking place for John Betjeman when he was secretary of Oxford Preservation Trust in the late 1940s; it became a key part of Oxford's music scene in the

1. **Mastiff and clock, Payne & Son, 131 High Street**

1960s and 1970s with a mighty juke box. The photographer Will R. Rose occupied the ground floor from 1909 to 1964, and he was also next door at no. 133 from 1916. Rose commissioned the four storey stone-fronted building here (1937, G.T. Gardner) on an incredibly narrow site, and you can pick out his name on the second floor ironwork balcony. Again, you can see how the building line envisaged the eventual widening of this end of High Street.

No. 132 High Street may date back to c.1500 when Richard Kent acquired the property and erected the Chequers inn at the rear. The three storey timber-framed front is rendered and the upper floors have sash windows above a massive first floor jetty. A passageway on the east side of the house leads down to the Chequers which we shall see later in the walk. Payne & Son's promotional mastiff and clock sit comfortably atop the silversmith's shop front which extends across the Chequers passage. Payne's was founded in Wallingford in 1790, and opened here in 1889 after George Septimus Payne purchased the business of Thomas Sheard, jeweller and watchmaker. The four storey stuccoed and timber-framed building may date back to the 18th century, but the frontage has been much altered with three-sided bays to the first and second floors and a moulded cornice at the parapet level.

The shop front that Taunt photographed in 1911 is still recognizable, but modern signage has replaced bold wooden letters, leaving just the number '131'.

The next five buildings, nos. 126–30, formed an almost improbably picturesque group until the late 19th century. No. 130 dates from the late 15th or early 16th century, and the front part is a two storey roughcast timber-framed building with two gables and cellars; the portion at the back was heightened in the 17th century, and rebuilt in 1930. No. 130 was owned from c.1600 by William Boswell (d.1638), a mercer who was elected Mayor of Oxford in 1622 and Alderman in 1627. In 1637, Alderman Boswell built for himself a fine new house behind no. 130 which we shall see later. At his death, he left both properties to his son, Dr William Boswell (d.1678), who had successfully made the transition from Town to Gown. Throughout the 19th century, and until 1929, the Carter family ran an open-fronted fish shop at these premises. Oxford Preservation Trust dissuaded the City from condemning the building and it was restored and partially rebuilt by the tobacconists, Fribourg and Treyer, who traded here until the 1970s.

The delightful nos. 127–29 High Street and the old Wheatsheaf pub were demolished in 1896 for the present over-sized building (1897) which is unconvincingly medieval despite its oriel windows, barge-boarded gables and half-timbering. Gill & Co., the ironmongers, who traced their origins back centuries, moved to these premises from no. 5 High Street in 1925, and traded here until the 1940s when they retreated to no. 127a in Wheatsheaf Yard. For a genuine ancient building and a remarkable survivor, you need only to look next door at no. 126. This is a three storey timber-framed house of the late 15th century, perhaps built by Henry Mychegood (d.1501), Squire Bedel of the University. The large gable with ornamental bargeboards is original, but the building was re-fronted to create 'a piece of street architecture' in the late 17th century, probably by Robert Pauling, mercer, who was Mayor of Oxford in 1679. The upper floors have shallow bays with rounded corners and semi-circular headed windows, and there is a complicated pediment with another arched window tucked into the gable. Solicitors HMG Law occupy the rear of the premises, and the M in their name maintains a tenuous link with Thomas Mallam who was in business at no. 126 as a tobacconist and auctioneer by 1823; later members of his family were solicitors here from 1875.

Formerly one of Oxford's great inns, the Bear occupied the site of nos. 123–25 High Street. Known as the Tabard in 1432,

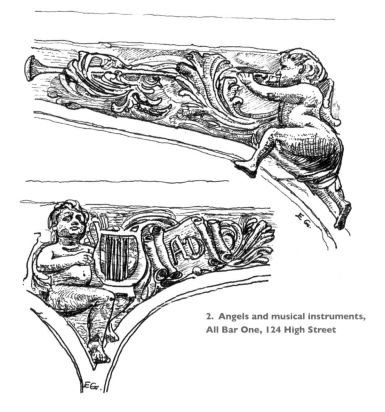

2. Angels and musical instruments, All Bar One, 124 High Street

and as the Bear by 1457, the inn was the equal of the Star by the mid 16th century, and similar in size to the Mitre opposite. Its premises extended down Alfred Street to Blue Boar Street. The inn was rebuilt in 1790, creating the existing three storey façade which is of stuccoed timber-framing with a continuous eaves cornice and parapet above sash windows. Although the coaching era was then at its height, the Bear was sold in 1801, and the premises were divided. James Russell began his music business at no. 125 in c.1850 before moving to no. 120 in the 1860s. Sydney Acott & Co., were music dealers at no. 124 from 1894, and eventually merged with Russell's in 1952 to create Russell Acott Ltd., at the same address. The music shop sold out to All Bar One in 1999, but you still enter the restaurant through Acott's 1912 shop front complete with carved angels playing musical instruments. No. 123 was briefly home to Oxford's first post office in 1841–2 before a fire packed it off to the Town Hall.

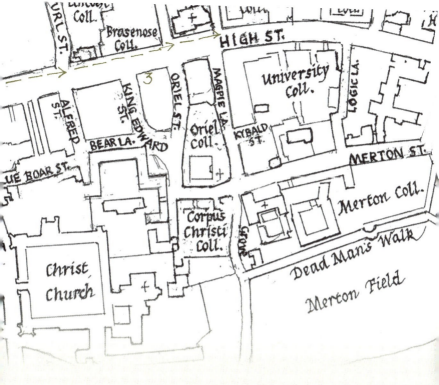

2 Alfred Street to Oriel Street

Alfred Street forms a narrow defile beyond the former Bear Inn. It was known as St Edward's Lane in c.1200 from St Edward's Church which stood near the site of the present Bear pub. The present name was in use by 1850 and probably derives from King Alfred, then still considered to be the founder of University College. An ornate corner turret with a conical roof introduces the Venetian Gothic former bank at nos. 120–22 High Street (1866–7, Horace Francis). This was a major commercial development on the site of the medieval Stodley's Inn, and a foretaste of the change that would soon transform the city's shopping streets. The spiky yellow brick building with stone dressings was built for the London and County Bank, a forerunner of the National Westminster Bank, which operated here until 2017. No. 120, to the left of the main entrance, was rented out separately as James Russell's music shop from 1867 until it merged with nearby Acott's in 1952. The shop front was then removed but it was reinstated (2018–19) to form the entrance to The Ivy restaurant.

In 1880, a letter found in the gutter outside the bank proved to be a political bombshell, leading to the unseating of Oxford's newly-elected Conservative MP, Alexander William Hall, and the disfranchising of the City for seven years. The letter exposed bribery and corruption at the heart of Hall's campaign, and the father of the boy who picked it up quickly passed it to the Mayor. Oxford Liberals gleefully lodged a petition against Hall, and an Oxford Election Commission was appointed, interviewing many local people and revealing 'a web of corruption on a quite unprecedented scale.' Fault was found with both parties, however, and Liberal hopes of benefiting from the scandal were dashed.

The large pedimented attic dormer on the Ede and Ravenscroft building next door provides a step down from no. 120 to the lower three storey properties beyond. It is a very characterful building rebuilt by Charles Prince, baker, in 1703, and has a three storey timber-framed front. The two first floor sash windows are pedimented to match the dormer which sits above a heavy moulded eaves cornice. The *Oxford Chronicle*, a Liberal-supporting newspaper, was printed and published at purpose-built premises behind no. 119 between 1874 and 1929. The well-known Oxford tailors, Hall Bros., occupied the shop from 1932 to 1995, and put in the splendid shop front with a double bow window (1930, G.T. Gardner). Hall's supplied Edward, Prince of Wales when he was at Magdalen College in 1912–14, and therefore displayed the royal warrant. In 1925, the firm was credited with introducing Oxford bags, flannels with very wide bottoms that became fashionable with undergraduates.

The future Edward VIII was also a regular visitor to Druce's chemist's shop next door at no. 118. George Claridge Druce (1850–1932), who was in business here from 1879 until his death, was also a well-known botanist and Mayor of Oxford in 1900; a blue plaque recording this link was unveiled in April 2018. The house may be 16th century in origin, and a major wall-painting dating back to c.1620–30 was discovered in an upstairs room in 1970. The three storey façade is a 19th century re-fronting of stuccoed timber-framing; the casement windows on the first and second floors have unusual semi-circular heads above the transoms.

The next two properties, nos. 116–17, are slightly taller. They were built as one in the 18th or early 19th century, and have stuccoed fronts with sash windows, eaves cornice and parapet. The Clarendon Press opened a central depository at no. 116 in 1875, and the Oxford University Press bookshop has been here since 1925. It expanded into no. 117 in 1997 when Lee & Ross Architects created a spectacular shop interior on two floors with residential accommodation for Lincoln College above. No.115 is of a similar date, again with a stuccoed front, but the upper floors have paired sash windows, and there is a distinctive modillioned eaves cornice below the parapet. Tom's Coffee

House flourished here from c.1759 to 1776, providing a general room at the front and a dons' sanctum known as the House of Lords at the back. James Wyatt (1774–1853) was a print-seller here by 1811, and he also served on the City Council for many years, being elected Mayor in 1842. The Pre-Raphaelite artists and their friends were regular visitors to Wyatt's, and Sir John Everett Millais (1829–96) painted James Wyatt with his granddaughter Mary here in 1849. Rowell & Son, jewellers, took over the premises in 1885, and traded here until 1986. The passageway beside the shop formerly led to the Long Room, home of the Oxford Union Society (founded in 1823) until a new debating hall, now the Old Library, was built behind Cornmarket Street in 1857.

Nos. 113–14 High Street were rebuilt for Lincoln College (1932–4, J.E. Thorpe) as a perfect foil for their older neighbours. The first and second floors have six sash windows with glazing bars, and there are two three-light sash windows in attic dormers above the cornice and parapet. The central first floor windows and the dormers are pedimented, perhaps as a deliberate echo of no. 119. John Bowell, draper and Mayor of Oxford in 1680, occupied an earlier property on this site, and Anthony Wood recorded that the chemist Peter Sthael built his 'elaboratory' in the former academic hall behind the shop in c.1663.

Beyond no. 113, there is a sudden change of character and scale as you reach the four storey buildings of white brick with stone dressings (1873, Frederick Codd) which announce King Edward Street. David Hunter-Blair recalled John Ruskin's reaction when he first saw this development: 'The hoardings had just been removed, and I awaited the inevitable explosion. The Slade Professor paused, surveyed the squalid vista, audibly muttered, "Damnable, simply damnable!" and strode on his way'. The Oriel College scheme created a wide new road to the college in what became Oriel Square and it provided shops and houses that could be let at commercial rents. Five High Street properties had to be demolished, three of them medieval houses that were recorded in detail by the artist, architect and antiquarian, John Chessell Buckler. Swan Court, running south to Bear Lane from the former Swan inn, was also cleared. Two High Street traders affected by the redevelopment moved into the new shops, William Way, grocer, at no. 110, and John Goundrey, ironmonger, at no. 109 on the corner of King Edward Street. Way's closed down in c.1907, just before the arrival of multiple stores began to hit High Street's independent food retailers. The old-established tailors, Standen & Co., moved into no. 110, but Wilton Woodward Ltd. (est. 1880) took over the premises in the early 1920s. Arthur Shepherd (est. 1877), tailors in Cornmarket Street, merged with Woodward's at the end of 1927 to form Shepherd and Woodward Ltd., based here. The new firm stressed that 'Oxford

3. Tackley's Inn, rear elevation from an old drawing, 106–7 High Street

leads as a centre for men's correct wear' and expanded into no. 109; in 1954, it also took in no. 113.

No. 108 High Street (1873, Frederick Codd), on the opposite corner of King Edward Street, was much more elaborately decorated for Hitchcock and Sons, chemists. Stone piers rise to the level of the shop fascia which still has its ornamental iron cresting. Hitchcock's were in business here until 1905, and chemists continued to occupy the premises until 1975.

The 19th century three storey fronts of nos. 106–7 provide no real clue as to the history of this remarkable building. No. 107 has two bay windows with casements on the first floor, and two sash windows above. No. 106 has two sets of three sash windows on the first and second floors, and two gabled dormers in the slate roof. These exteriors are picturesque enough, but they mask one of the very few surviving examples of a medieval academic hall which we shall explore later. Known as Tackley's Inn, it was built in c.1320 by Roger le Mareschal, parson of Tackley, presumably as a speculation. It was the first property that Adam de Brome acquired for the foundation of Oriel College in 1324, and the fledgling college briefly occupied the building before moving to its present site in 1329. As built, Tackley's Inn consisted of five shops on the street frontage, each with a solar above and access to a cellar below which would be leased to laymen. Behind this, and approached by a passage between the shops, there was a large hall and an inner chamber with a solar above, let to scholars.

Tackley's Inn has had many different uses over the years. In 1549, Oriel College – which still owns the property today – leased the hall and the shops to Garbrand Harkes, a Dutch Protestant refugee, who sold books from the ground floor and wine from the vaulted cellar. It continued to be a bookshop until the end of the 17th century, and then became Puffett's Coffee House. No. 106 was again a bookshop, Wheeler's, between c.1839 and 1918, and briefly became Wheeler & Day's photographic studio after the firm bought up Edward Bracher's business (at no. 26 opposite) in 1865, and took on Henry Taunt as photographic manager. No. 107 was a branch of Boffin's bakery and confectionery business between 1861 and 1906, and James Boffin probably inserted the first floor bay windows soon after he moved in. Boffin's reputation was such that even a clown at the circus hymned the firm's praises:

> Till I'm up to my eyes
> In Boffin's mince pies
> I'll never be happy again.

No. 105 stands well forward of its neighbour, making room for windows in the side elevation which provide enviable views along High Street. It dates back to the 17th century, and you can just glimpse the tops of two gables of the earlier house above the projecting eaves cornice which was part of the 18th century re-fronting. The four storey front is of stuccoed timber-framing with a large three-light sash window on the first floor, and two sash windows in each of the upper floors. The next property, no. 104, is 16th century in origin, but again it has a much later stuccoed timber-framed front, this time with a bay window on each floor and a prominent modillioned eaves cornice. The building was formerly the Salutation Inn, visited on several occasions by the historian and diarist, Anthony Wood, and it is still called Salutation House. It was a coffee house for much of the 18th century, and, by the mid 1840s, it was Charles Richards' bookshop and auction room. As a boy in the 1850s, Henry Taunt worked for Richards for a couple of years, reading many books during the vacations when 'things were very leisurely'. Since Richards' day, booksellers have always occupied the premises, although Sanders of Oxford – based here since 1927 – now specialize in maps and prints.

Nos. 102–3 High Street, and the first two houses in Oriel Street, were built as a single block between 1713 and 1738 by William Ives, apothecary. The High Street frontages are of stuccoed timber-framing, and both have been very satisfyingly altered over the years No. 103 is of four storeys with a seven-light window on the first floor and a three-light sash window on both the second and third floor; a timber balcony provides an unusual feature above the bold projecting modillioned eaves cornice. No. 102, on the corner, is three storeys high, and has Ionic pilasters beside the three-light sash window on the first floor, and a pediment above the second floor window. From 1834 to 1890, this prominent site was occupied by Spiers & Son, dealers in fancy goods celebrated in Cuthbert Bede's Oxford novel, *The Adventures of Verdant Green*, published in 1853. Our hero, a freshman at the University, is soon attracted to the shop, and he emerges laden with artistic souvenirs for all the family. He buys a paper-knife for himself, and is rewarded by Mr Spiers with 'a perfect bijou of art, in the shape of "a memorial for visitors to Oxford", in which the chief glories of that city were set forth in gold and colours, in the most attractive form ...' Oscar Wilde followed this fictional lead while he was at Magdalen, running up a debt of almost £11 by buying such things as playing cards, Venetian glass and travelling cases. The Revd William Tuckwell recalled that the firm's 'display of papier mâché and of ceramic ware, surrounding a beautiful cardboard model of the Martyrs' Memorial, was one of the features in the 1851 Exhibition.' The growing popularity of photographic souvenirs eventually led to Spiers' decline and Adamson & Son, tailors, took over the whole block of buildings, including nos. 1–3 Oriel Street, until 1964.

Reaching Oriel Street, you come to the probable eastern limit of the original Saxon burh laid out in c.900. The first East Gate would have stood here, and it is argued that Oriel Street and St Mary's Passage, the former Schools Street, north of High Street, represent the road which would have been formed inside the ramparts. Today's Catte Street and Magpie Lane echo the line of the defensive ditch outside the ramparts. St Mary the Virgin Church is first recorded in 1086, but it seems likely that there was a Saxon church here occupying a similar position to the churches beside the North and South Gates in the town wall. That role would have ceased when the defended area of Oxford was extended to a new East Gate where the Eastgate Hotel now stands.

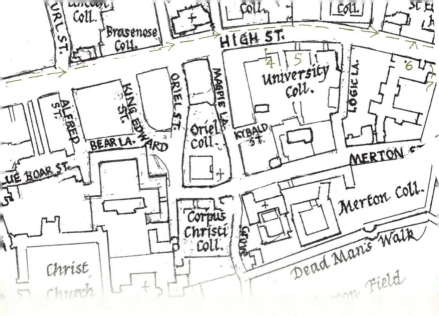

3 Oriel Street to Merton Street

Beyond Oriel Street, the Rhodes Building for Oriel College (1908–11, Basil Champneys) was another chapter in what the *Oxford Mail* saw in 1929 as the victory of education over commerce in High Street. Other major buildings, such as the Examination Schools and the Non-Collegiate Delegacy, had already changed the face of High Street, and T.G. Jackson's new front for Brasenose College almost opposite was completed while the Rhodes Building was under construction. Pevsner describes Champneys' building as 'a mighty piece, dominating its stretch of the High Street.' It is built of ashlar stone in a later 17th century style, three storeys high and nine bays wide, with a traditional central gate-tower. An inscription on the building acknowledges that it was paid for through a bequest by Cecil Rhodes (1853–1902), who had been an undergraduate at Oriel. The large letters in the inscription form a chronogram which identifies the date of construction as 1911 in Roman numerals. A rather unheroic statue of the imperialist and diamond mining entrepreneur Cecil Rhodes, in jacket and trousers and holding his hat, is set high up on the gate-tower, well above the statues of Edward VII, George V and college worthies in their first floor niches.

The Rhodes Building was listed in 1972 and re-graded II* in 2011, and there were unsuccessful objections on architectural grounds to Oriel's roof-top additions (2010, Marcus Beale Architects). For many years, however, the building had been loathed, and W. E. Sherwood complained in 1927 that Oriel had 'broken out into the High ... destroying a most picturesque group of old houses in so doing and, to put it gently, hardly compensating us for their removal'. Seven buildings, nos. 95–101 High Street, were lost, including houses and shops in front of St Mary's Hall which dated back to 1397. No. 96 was the former home of Alderman John Nixon (c.1589–1662), mercer and Mayor of Oxford in 1636, 1646 and 1654. He was among the 'puritanical tradesmen' who fled the city during the Civil War, and he gave evidence at Archbishop William Laud's trial in 1644, testifying that he had seen from his window passers-by pausing outside Laud's new porch at St Mary the Virgin Church, and 'doing outrageous homage to its statue of the crowned Virgin Mary holding the infant Christ'. Among his many charitable activities, he founded Nixon's School for the sons of poor freemen in 1658 and this continued in the Town Hall yard until the 1890s. The house that he shared with his wife, Joan (d.1671) had a three storey timber-framed front ornamented with decorative plasterwork. Back in c.1520, the front shop at this property was occupied by the bookseller, John Dorne.

Beyond Magpie Lane, the brick and half-timbered four storey front of no. 94 High Street is a riotous exercise in mock Tudor (1902, Davy & Salter). There are oriel windows to the first floor, casement windows on the upper floors, and a wooden roof-top balcony; the arms of Queen Elizabeth are displayed between the first floor windows. This frontage masks a much older house, which we shall see later in Magpie Lane. Joseph Vincent, stationer, was the first occupant of the reconstructed no. 92, and Hall Bros., tailors, had their shop here between 1909 and 1931 when they moved to no. 119. No. 94 is now part of the Old Bank Hotel, but Barclays Bank only occupied this corner property for a few years before the bank closed in 1998. William Fletcher (1739–1826) and John Parsons (1752–1814), both mercers, went into partnership as bankers in 1775 and they built no. 93 as their first premises, adding no. 92 in 1798. Both properties are four storeys high and built of ashlar stone. The rusticated ground floor, with six semi-circular arched recessed windows and three similar doorways, is common to both properties, but the first floor sash windows at no. 93 have semi-circular heads while those next door have pediments; no. 92 also has a very prominent modillioned and dentilled cornice. The name Old Bank was introduced in about 1790 to distinguish the business from newer rivals in the city. According to the Revd William Tuckwell, the bank successfully negotiated the money panic of 1825 and its reputation was such that it secured the deposits of every Oxford college. Barclays absorbed the firm in 1900, but kept the Old Bank branch open until 1998. The buildings were successfully converted into a hotel and restaurant in 1999.

In 2006, the Old Bank Hotel expanded eastward into no. 91 High Street, a branch of the National Provincial, later the National Westminster Bank until 1975. The four storey building dates from c.1800 and it was a grand private house until the early 20th century. It has a stuccoed timber-framed front with sash windows above an ashlar stone ground floor. No. 90 is again four storeys high and of stuccoed timber-framing, with a canted bay window on each of the upper floors; there is a Doric column at each side of the ground floor shop. James Adam, cabinet maker, added this frontage in c.1812 to modernize and enlarge a fine timber-framed house built in 1612 by John Williams, apothecary. Williams' building was probably intended as a private nursing home for country gentry, close to Oxford doctors, and the interior retains fine original panelling and fireplaces. The Jacobean frontage also survives behind the present one. Arthur Tillyard, another apothecary, opened a coffee house here in 1655 which was frequented in its early days by scientists who went on to found the Royal Society in London. John Ruskin's mother lodged here while he was an undergraduate at Christ Church between 1836 and 1840. By that time, Joseph Vincent had moved his bookshop and publishing house, to no. 90, and his son, also Joseph, published the *Oxford University and City Herald* here until 1892. Walter Bradford Woodgate founded Vincent's Club, a club for elite sportsmen, in an upstairs room in 1863, and, for want of a better name, named it after the landlord. University College acquired the property in 1905 and converted it into student accommodation.

New Building (1842, Sir Charles Barry) next to no. 90 was the product of earlier expansionism after University College asked the architect to design a new building 'in keeping with that of the College.' The ashlar stone building in Tudor Gothic style is three storeys high and three bays wide. It has been variously described as plain, seemly or staid, and its most appealing features are the bay windows richly decorated with coats of arms. J.M.W. Turner's famous painting of the High Street (1810), displayed in the Ashmolean Museum, depicts the previous building on the site, the former Three Tuns tavern. This four storey three-gabled timber-framed building was built in 1642, and its rich ornamentation and plasterwork decoration bore witness to Oxford's prosperity on the eve of the Civil War. Stanton Hall, an academic hall, had flourished here in the 14th and 15th centuries, and elements of that building were perhaps incorporated into the Three Tuns. The tavern was a prominent meeting-place for Oxford clubs and All Souls' dons until c.1750, but the

4. Shelley Memorial dome in street scene, University College

ground floor had been divided into two shops by the late 1830s when artists recorded the threatened building.

Beyond the New Building, you reach a surprising gap in the otherwise continuous street frontage where a dome rises behind a stone wall. University College had demolished Deep Hall on this site in c.1810, and Charles Buckeridge prepared plans for a new building here in 1866. Nothing came of that project, and the domed building (1893, Basil Champneys) housing Edward Onslow Ford's sculpture of the poet, Percy Bysshe Shelley, eventually occupied the site. Shelley had been expelled by the College in 1811 for circulating an atheistic pamphlet and was not therefore an obvious candidate for a prominent memorial, but Lady Shelley, the poet's daughter-in-law, persuaded the governing body to accept a statue that she had originally commissioned for his grave in Rome. The College considered but chose not to proceed with a proposal by the architect, A.S.G. Butler, to build over the Shelley Memorial in the 1920s and the dome survived. A plaque on the stone wall recalls that the scientists, Robert Boyle (1627–91) and Robert Hooke (1635–1703), lodged and set up a laboratory in a building on this site between 1655 and 1668. The building was the former Deep Hall, a medieval academic hall that was then leased to Matthew or John Cross, an apothecary. Boyle and Hooke successfully designed a modern air pump, and Hooke created the compound microscope, enabling him to identify biological cells for the first time.

And so we reach the monumental High Street façade of University College (Univ), three storeys high, 23 bays long and boasting two gate-towers. The story that King Alfred founded the College in 872 is now discredited, but Univ can still claim to be the oldest college in Oxford since the scholar William of Durham (d.1249) left money for its foundation. The College had a precarious early existence in buildings on the site now occupied by Brasenose, and only moved to High Street in the mid-14th century. At first, Univ simply took over an existing hall, but a quadrangle much smaller than the present one was built between the 1390s and 1473. This sufficed until the 1630s when the need to house growing numbers of undergraduates led to the building of the Front Quadrangle (1634-76, Richard Maude). Work on the west range, which required no demolition of college buildings, began in 1634 and the High Street front was built between 1635 and 1637. However, the Civil War and its aftermath checked progress, and the college resembled a building site for years. The public face of the Front Quadrangle is set high above High Street, apparently as an insurance against flooding. Each bay is marked

5. Queen Anne's statue, University College gate–tower

by a small gable, and the square-headed windows on each floor are linked by a continuous string course. The gate-tower rises to an embattled parapet, and a first floor niche contains a statue of Queen Anne, seemingly in pugnacious mood; it was installed there in 1709 to replace a figure of King Alfred.

David Loggan's 1675 bird's eye view of University College shows two older buildings between the Main Quadrangle and Logic Lane, which the historian Herbert Hurst described as 'the quaintest objects in the whole High Street.' They were Little University Hall which the College had taken over as the Master's Lodging in 1531, and the Cock on the Hoop, later the Half Moon, a large property on the corner of Logic Lane. These buildings were demolished in 1716 for Univ's Radcliffe Quadrangle (1716–19), following a bequest by John Radcliffe (1650–1714), a member of the College who had amassed a fortune through his successful career as a doctor. He left instructions that the new quad should be 'answerable to the front already built', and it is therefore a virtual replica of the Front Quad, 80 years later. The statue facing the street in the central gate-tower is of Queen Mary II.

Durham Building (1903, H.W. Moore) represented the expansion of Univ east of Logic Lane. The High Street front is of ashlar stone, four bays wide and three storeys high. The outer bays have two-storeyed oriel windows and gables above their crenellated parapets. Nos. 87–88 High Street on this site were originally Sheld Hall in the early 15th century, and had become the home of a doctor, Richard Slythurst (d.1587) by 1575 when an overmantel with the initials RS and MS was installed. Both this feature and fine contemporary panelling of moralizing scenes saved from this building were subsequently placed in the College's Summer Common Room. The building later became a pub, the Saracen's Head or Alfred's Head and, from c.1800, had a four storey stuccoed timber-framed front with sash windows on the upper floors. From 1868, Univ used it as an annexe for students called University Hall.

A little stone bridge (1905, H.W. Moore) connects Durham Building with the Radcliffe Quadrangle across Logic Lane. It is an inconspicuous structure, unlike its grander cousin, Hertford's Bridge of Sighs, but Univ was only able to build it after a bitter two-year legal dispute with the City. The argument revolved around the ownership of Logic Lane, which was ultimately awarded to the College, leaving the City to pay costs of £3,000.

Beyond Durham Building, you come to nos. 86–87 High Street, a house dating back to the early 17th century, but built on the site of Bostar Hall, a medieval academic hall. Bostar Hall was at the heart of the scheme by William Waynflete, Bishop of Winchester, to found Magdalen Hall in 1448. Waynflete negotiated for properties on both sides, but eventually dissolved his hall in 1458 and moved on to his grander vision for Magdalen College. The present building has a three storey roughcast timber-framed front with three sash windows in each upper floor and an overhang at the second floor. It was probably built by Richard Radcliffe and served as a private nursing home for many years; medicinal plants would have been grown in large gardens to the rear. The local builder, John Plowman, built the fine ashlar stone ground floor with seven Doric columns when he leased the property in 1832, and it now forms a magnificent shop front. Univ bought the property from Magdalen College in 1884 and has used the upper floors for student accommodation since 1949. No. 85 next door, occupied by Antiques on High since 1998, was another Univ acquisition, this time from the Queen's College, and the upper floors have housed students since 1946. The building is probably 17th or 18th century in origin, but the four storey front of stuccoed timber-framing dates from the 18th century. There are two sash windows in each of the upper floors and a modern double-sash window in the attic above the eaves cornice.

The next two properties, nos. 83–84 High Street, are all that remain of the Angel, Oxford's principal inn from the late 17th century until it closed in 1866. The inn had small beginnings as the Tabard in 1418, but it had been enlarged and re-named the Angel by the early 16th century. The closure of Kybald Street behind the Angel in 1442 enabled the inn to extend its stabling and service buildings south into Merton Street. The Angel seems to have been rebuilt or enlarged in 1663, and, at the height of its prosperity during the coaching era, the inn also took over nos. 83–84, properties which have belonged to University College since the early 14th century.

Richard Costar, landlord of the Angel, leased no. 84 in 1813, and rebuilt the premises over the next decade with bedrooms and sitting-rooms upstairs and a pillared coffee-room, today's Grand Café, on the ground floor. The result was this four storey stuccoed building, but without the elaborate ground floor shop front with Corinthian pilasters which was a later addition. When these two buildings were part of the Angel, they had no direct access to the High Street, and could only be reached by way of the inn's main entrance to the east. No. 84 has an iron balcony and two tall semi-circular arched window-frames with casement windows on the first floor. Each of the upper floors has two sash windows, those on the third floor being located above a moulded cornice.

No. 83 also has a four storey stuccoed front, dating perhaps from the late 18th or early 19th century, but it is more ornate than its neighbour, with a moulded cornice and two Composite pilasters, the caps of which are carved with heads of Bacchus. The first floor has an iron balcony and a three-light Venetian window. There are two sash windows above a stone band on the second floor, and two blind sash windows, which must post-date the Window Tax, above the cornice on the third floor.

Princes and dukes lodged at the Angel in the late 17th century and Queen Adelaide, the consort of William IV, stayed there in 1835. The official reception in her apartment prompted some amusement in University circles when the Mayor, unfamiliar with royal etiquette, shook her hand instead of kissing it! Nine coaches to different destinations left the Angel at 8 a.m. every day in the 1830s and many vehicles would have clattered down to the stables in Merton Street each day. William Costar (d. 1802) was landlord of the Angel and stage-coach proprietor for many years, and his son Richard (1765–1840) had over 300 horses at work. From 1585, the Angel, and the Greyhound on the corner of Longwall Street, leased meadows north-east of Magdalen Bridge from Magdalen College, presumably to provide hay and grazing for their own, as well as customers', horses; the area is still known today as Angel and Greyhound Meadow.

In 1829, when fast stage-coach services along much-improved turnpike roads were still unchallenged by the railways, Samuel Young Griffith paid £22,500 for the lease of the Angel. In 1855, with the coaching business in terminal decline, he tried to sell the inn, but he was only able to offload the Univ properties, nos. 83 and 84. The purchaser was Francis Thomas Cooper (1811–62), a grocer on the north side of High Street who now moved his shop and home to no. 84, and let out no. 83. His son, Frank Cooper (1844–1927), inherited the business in 1867 and expanded into the shop next door where, as noted by a blue plaque, Frank's wife, Sarah Cooper, first made 76 pounds of marmalade in 1874, and sold the surplus in the shop. It proved so popular that production of what was commonly called 'squish' rose to 340 pounds in 1875 and to 100,000 pounds in 1902 before the company opened the Victoria Works in Park End Street. Frank Cooper retained this central shop until 1919 and, in the 1980s, there was a short-lived Frank Cooper museum at no. 84.

No. 84 is also interesting as the site of the first coffee house in England, opened in 1650 or 1651 by Jacob, a Jew. In the late 18th century, the building was the family home and business premises of James Sadler (1753-1828), pastry cook, chemist, and England's first aeronaut in 1784. The Oxford & District Co-operative Society Ltd., opened the Angel café in the former coffee-room in 1943, and a tablet designed by Lawrence Dale was unveiled inside the café in 1952, recording Jacob's pioneering

6. Dragon boot–scrapers outside Examination Schools

coffee house. The Angel café closed in the mid 1950s, but reopened as the Grand Café in 1997.

Magdalen College sold its portion of the Angel Hotel to the University in 1866 for new Examination Schools, that were needed because of increasing student numbers and a growing reliance on written rather than oral examinations. The Schools duly ousted nos. 77–82 High Street, but nos. 83–84 survived because they were in different ownership, and peripheral to the development. In 1876, Thomas Graham Jackson won an informal limited competition to design the new building, his choice of an eclectic style which became known as 'Anglo-Jackson' being preferred to his rivals' Gothic. The Examination Schools (1876–82) were the first of many Oxford buildings designed by Jackson, and his choice of Clipsham stone from Rutland was also highly significant for the future of the city's built environment. The High Street front reflects Jackson's 'haunting vision of Elizabethan and Jacobean work, and especially those long mullioned and transomed windows at Kirby Hall'. It is five bays wide with an elaborately carved central porch, supported on Ionic pillars and adorned with carvings of a *vivâ voce* examination and the conferment of degrees. The outer bays project slightly, and feature a spacious mullioned window and an arcaded parapet. A tall and elaborately designed louvre rises from the Stonesfield slate roof. The overall impression is spectacular, but Pevsner remarked that the building presents a daunting image of examination, pitting 'puny candidates' against 'the moloch of the testing machinery'. In both World Wars, the Examination Schools were converted into a military hospital. Traffic permitting, you may like to cross the street here to view the dragon boot-scrapers beside the entrance, a relic of muddy roads, and to appreciate the carvings above the door.

The University employed Jackson again to design what is now the Ruskin School of Art on the corner

7. Carved frieze detail, squirrels, foliage and date-stone, Ruskin School of Art

of High Street and Merton Street. The building (1886–8), on the sites of nos. 74–76 High Street, was built for the Delegacy of Unattached Students and Jackson chose an elaborate Tudor Gothic style to set it apart from the Examination Schools. The High Street front of Doulting stone has three gabled bays with upper windows and panel tracery on the first floor. The panels provided space for Jackson to include his name, college – he was a former Fellow of Wadham – and the fact that he had erected the building. The plain ground floor has a small Elizabethan doorway and, above it, there is a delightful frieze of carved birds and animals which repays close inspection. The Delegacy of Unattached, later Non-Collegiate, Students remained here until 1936 and the Ruskin School has occupied the building since 1975.

4 Merton Street to Magdalen Bridge

Between Merton Street and Longwall Street, High Street narrowed considerably until 1771 when the Oxford Improvement Act led swiftly to the demolition of the East Gate and other encroaching properties. High Street was widened at this point to form a regular approach to the new Magdalen Bridge, and subsequent buildings had to respect that building line; in some cases, existing properties were set back and re-fronted. No. 73 High Street, on the corner of Merton Street, was entirely rebuilt, and became the Flying Horse pub until c.1876. It was then re-named the Eastgate Hotel and that name was retained when the present building (1900, E.P. Warren) was erected. Warren's building was a very tactful insertion, with mullioned and transomed windows, and a tall brick chimney stack and two dormers providing an interesting roof line. A cartouche at first floor level illustrates the East Gate as it appeared in the 18th century.

The medieval East Gate was a much more substantial structure, and probably consisted of a square gate

8. Cartouche on Eastgate Hotel

tower flanked by two smaller square towers. Holy Trinity Chapel, situated in a room above the gate, was granted to St Frideswide's Priory in 1122 and the priory gave it to the Trinitarian Friars in c.1310. Mayors returning to Oxford visited the chapel to give thanks for a safe journey before being greeted outside by fellow-townsmen. Loggan in 1675 still showed two square towers, and the East Gate with a round-headed archway shown on the cartouche was probably the result of the City's decision in 1711 to demolish the decayed original and 'make the passage there "hansome and ornamentall"'.

Nos. 71–72 High Street, next to the Eastgate Hotel, emerged from the radical re-shaping of the area in the 1770s. Originally one building, it has a four storey plastered timber-framed front with three-light sash windows on the upper floors and a modillioned eaves cornice. By 1851, these premises were occupied as shops with living accommodation above. The adjoining property, nos. 69–70, is a three storey 18th century building with a modern stuccoed front, and sash windows above the shop front. Look more closely, however, and you will see quoins at both ends of the ground floor, key stones above the doorways, and the brackets which supported a cornice over the door to no. 69. Until 1933, this was a high-quality brick house with stone dressings, unusual in Oxford, but the front was then rendered on the initiative of Magdalen College's Estates Bursar. The Governing Body 'very faithfully criticised' him for what was described in 1935 as 'probably the worst example of needless spoliation that an old house in Oxford has suffered'. Given the alignment of the building, it is likely to date from the 1770s, but internal panelling is thought to date from the mid 18th century. Both halves of the property were originally private houses, but no. 69 was already a shop by 1839, and Charles Laker, grocer, lived there above his shop from c.1851 to 1899. He was a member of Oxford Local Board, a highways and sanitary body, for many years and its last Chairman in 1888–9.

No. 68, with its four storey half-timbered front and a half-hipped roof, was rebuilt in the late 19th century by James Jenkin (1827–98), Laker's rival as a grocer from c.1862, and Mayor of Oxford in 1881–2. Jenkin's shop and later businesses extended into the very different no. 67, hence the handsome modern shop front that spans both properties. Nos. 66–67 High Street were built as a pair of three storey houses of stuccoed rubble, perhaps as early as c.1700. Each floor has a three-light sash window and there are two dormers in the hipped roof. No. 66 and subsequent properties have always been private houses or lodging-houses, and they retain original doorways with fanlights. No. 65 probably dates from the late 18th century and has a four storey stuccoed timber-framed front with a three-light sash window on each floor. Since 1984, Stanford House has occupied this building and nos. 66–70 to enable students from Stanford University in California to spend one or two terms in Oxford as part of their degree course.

The next house, no. 64, is a late 18th century three storey ashlar stone house, with bands at each floor and a parapet. The first floor sash windows have rectangular recessed panels above them, and between each window there is an oval patera or ornament. William Tuckwell, surgeon, occupied this very fine private house in the 1830s, and the building is significant in the local history of photography as the first home of Edward Bracher's Daguerrotype Institution in 1844 before he moved to more central premises at no. 26 High Street. No. 63 is another ashlar stone house, a storey higher than its neighbour. It has a rusticated ground floor, a good iron balcony on the first floor and two sash windows with keystones on each of the upper floors. With no. 62, we are back to stuccoed timber-framing, another four storey house of c.1800 particularly distinguished by a wooden cornice at the first and third floors, and its first floor iron grille.

No. 61, Magdalen Gate House, was built in 1802 for Thomas Roberson, Oxford's Town Clerk between 1825 and 1839. The north elevation is a little unprepossessing with three blind windows to each floor and a stone band between each storey. Soon, however, you have a fine view across the road towards the principal east elevation, a three storey ashlar stone façade with a pediment containing a circular lunette window. Blind boxes above the long casement windows on the first floor are a reminder that blinds would have been needed to protect furnishings from damage in this glorious sun trap. Roberson was declared bankrupt in 1810, and he was forced to sell the property. Later occupants have included Dr George Williams (d.1834), Sherardian Professor of Botany between 1796 and 1834, and Charles Cannan (d.1919), Secretary to the Delegates of the Oxford University Press.

We have now reached Rose Lane, formerly Trinity Lane. The earlier name, still current in the early 17th century, recalled the Trinitarian Friars who began trying to establish a house in Oxford in 1286. Edmund, Earl of Cornwall, granted them land south of High Street outside the East Gate in 1293 and, by renting vacant land beneath the town wall, they secured the whole block between the East Gate and Trinity Lane. Their property passed to Edward III in c.1351 after the Black Death swept away the friars, and Richard II granted it to the town in 1391. The buildings were occupied as Trinity Hall by secular and religious scholars who paid rent to the town. Robert Perrot of Magdalen College acquired the premises in 1546 and later converted part into a barn and stable and the rest into houses for four poor almsmen who begged around Oxford as 'Trinity Men.' In the early 17th century, the area was said to contain 'certaine poor Cottages and scattering Houses, unto the gate of Trinitie Lane.' Loggan in 1675 suggests that these houses lay behind the present building line, but most properties had encroached further forward by 1771.

John Gwynn surveyed the area around Magdalen Bridge in 1771 to indicate which buildings would have to be demolished or set back in order to form an adequate approach to his proposed bridge. East of

Rose Lane, High Street, or Bridge Street as this part was then known, narrowed from 38 to 33 feet, and finally to 27 feet where the Professor of Botany's house and library stood opposite Magdalen Tower. Beginning at Rose Lane, you would have seen the Noah's Ark pub and several old houses before reaching the entrance to the Botanic Garden. This area had been known as Noah's Ark, an ironic reference to regular flooding, since at least the 15th century when St John's Hospital (1231–1457), a medieval religious foundation on the site of Magdalen College, acquired the land. Beyond Noah's Ark, the Botanic Garden entrance was on the site of the Jews' cemetery. The Jewish community in Oxford had acquired land for a cemetery outside the East Gate in c.1180, which straddled both sides of the street, but Henry III granted away the northern portion in 1231 to create a site for St John's Hospital. The strip of land opposite was used as the Jewish cemetery until Edward I expelled the last Jews from the country in 1290. St John's Hospital continued to use the site for burials until the institution was hurriedly dissolved in 1457 to make way for William Waynflete's Magdalen College. The Botanic Garden was not directly threatened by road widening in the 1770s, but the Professor of Botany's house obstructed the new Magdalen Bridge and it was demolished in 1790.

Continue on to Magdalen Bridge past the now rather scabrous Chancellor's milestone at the foot of Magdalen Tower. It probably dates from the 1770s, and marked your arrival in Oxford during the turnpike road era. The eroded text advises you that you are 54 miles from London and 8½ miles from Woodstock. On June 13th, 1814, the Prince Regent stepped down from his carriage near here during a spectacular royal visit to celebrate the signing of the Treaty of Paris that brought a short-lived peace with France. He was greeted by Lord Grenville, Chancellor of the University, and the Mayor, Joseph Lock, and they led a procession of members of the University and councillors along a High Street crowded with spectators. Allied sovereigns and generals arrived later by carriage, and one enterprising local shoemaker tossed a pair of new boots into Prince Blücher's vehicle so that he could claim to be supplier to the Prussian field marshal. The Chancellor hosted a grand dinner for the Prince Regent and foreign dignitaries in the Radcliffe Camera. Afterwards, the visitors were received at the Town Hall and the Town Clerk, William Elias Taunton, read a welcoming address on behalf of the council. The Prince Regent knighted him, apparently mistaking him for the Mayor, whom he also knighted!

The building of Gwynn's Magdalen Bridge (1772–9) was a huge undertaking, involving the formation of a temporary road via Cowley Place and Milham

Meadow to Rose Lane. The elegant stone bridge with large semi-circular arches and plain balustrades replaced a decayed medieval and later structure. There has been a bridge here across the river Cherwell since at least 1004, known sometimes as East Bridge or Pettypont (little bridge) to distinguish it from the Grandpont across the Thames flood plain south of Oxford. Magdalen Bridge had to be widened by 12 feet on the southern side in 1882–3 to accommodate growing traffic and particularly the horse trams which had just been introduced. Its appearance was much enhanced (1989–93) when an Oxford Preservation Trust fund-raising campaign enabled Oxfordshire County Council to renew cast concrete balusters in natural stone and lay stone paving. Having come so far, you will probably wish to enjoy views of Angel and Greyhound Meadow set between branches of the river Cherwell before returning to Longwall Street and crossing to the south side of High Street at the traffic lights.

5 Eastgate Hotel to Merton College

The network of narrow streets and alleys south of High Street provides a highly enjoyable, if circuitous, way of getting back to Carfax. As is so often the case in central Oxford, this townscape has evolved much more over the centuries than you might expect. We begin by turning left past the Eastgate Hotel into Merton Street, a surviving section of the roadway inside the Saxon ramparts and the later city walls that was originally needed for defensive purposes. This north-south portion of Merton Street was known as King Street in the 18th and 19th centuries and as Coach and Horses Lane in 1772, presumably from the local pub of that name. As the medieval defences became obsolete, the City was happy to let vacant land inside the walls for house-building, as happened here by the mid 17th century on the left hand side of the street. Large sections of the intra-mural roadway were also acquired by expanding halls and colleges, and this part of Merton Street would originally have been about twice as long, continuing south to the city wall in what is now Merton College Fellows' Garden, before heading west towards the South Gate in St Aldate's.

Although you are exploring a street that probably dates back to the early 11th century, you will see no trace of great

9. Red rose on Merton Street screen to Examination Schools

antiquity. The local historian, Harry Paintin, recalled a very different King Street with old houses 'of the irregular and undulating character that was once so attractive a feature of domestic work in Oxford'. Demolition for the Examination Schools began the physical transformation of the street in the 1870s, although Thomas Hill refused to give up his lease and remained in his house on the building site until c.1880. On your left, beyond the side elevation of the original Eastgate Hotel (1900, E. P. Warren), you come to three large houses (1904, A. Mardon Mowbray) built for Magdalen College dons, which now form part of Mercure Hotels Oxford Eastgate. Further along the street, Merton College had already built three dons' houses (1902, E. P. Warren) faced with stone and roughcast stucco to match the Eastgate. On your right, Jackson's Non-Collegiate Delegacy (1886–8) is followed by his Examination Schools (1876-82), a veritable stately home set in an open quadrangle behind an ornamental iron screen with ashlar stone piers; notice the red rose detail on the ironwork. The Merton Street front has a central 'tower of the orders', and two large projecting wings, the North and South Schools, each of which terminates with a six-light window with a pediment and a small Venetian window in the gable. First floor plaques on the South School proudly boast: *Veritas Liberabit* (Truth will set free) and *Bonitas Regnabit* (Goodness will rule).

Beyond the Examination Schools, a now largely vanished medieval street, variously known as Kybald Street, Harehall Lane or Nightingale Lane, ran west across Logic Lane to Magpie Lane. It was laid out in c.1130, and first recorded as Kybald Street in c.1212; its other names derived from academic halls. Henry VI ordered the closure of the east end of the street in 1447 following allegations that it 'gave occasion to Night Walkers and Varlets to commit several Robberies and outcries therein…' William Waynflete's plans to establish Magdalen Hall in the area probably lay behind all this.

Turn right at the corner, and into the part of Merton Street that has successfully resisted the tide of tarmac which gradually engulfed most city-centre roads. The cobbled street surface is a jarring experience for cyclists, and not very pedestrian friendly, but it provides a fine visual setting for historic buildings on both sides. Merton Street was first known as St John's Street from c.1200 after the former parish church in what is now Merton College Chapel, and the present name is not recorded until 1772. Note the Warden of Merton's Lodgings on the corner, originally designed by Carden & Godfrey, and built in 1966. They were a more compact, but never admired, replacement for the 1908 lodgings nearer the College and blocked a wonderful view of Magdalen Tower. In an echo of Merton's earlier controversy over Butterfield's Grove Building, they now have a 'chastened' ashlar stone and rendered front (2010, Acanthus Clews Architects). South of the lodgings, and over the splendid rubble stone wall with its ironwork defences, you can glimpse a stone summer-house (1706–7) built in the College garden. The ancient wall running west towards St Alban Hall forms the boundary of Merton College Fellows' Garden. Eight houses and academic halls occupied this frontage until the 14th century, but they were then abandoned as Oxford's population declined, and Merton gradually acquired the sites. A blocked doorway in the wall, often obscured by parked cars, would have provided access to one of these properties.

In 1611, Merton College leased from the City a long strip of land beside the city wall which formed the site of a handsome terraced walk laid out in 1711. At this time, Merton's gardens were a popular attraction, thronged with undergraduates and their ladies on Sunday evenings. John Dry resorted to poetry to praise the gardens' 'soft Recesses' and 'cool Retreats', and the many 'charming Nymphs' who adorned them. Nicholas Amherst published a curmudgeonly response, depicting colleges that swarmed with 'Consummate Coxcombs' and remarking on the 'Multitude of Female Residentiaries who have of late infested our Learned Retirements, and drawn off Numbers of unwary young Persons from their studies.' Merton College clearly shared Amherst's jaundiced view and closed the gardens to the public in 1718.

Opposite the Fellows' Garden, nos. 13–18 Merton Street – all now owned by University College – form an attractive group of town houses. No. 18, on the corner, has a 19th century three storey stuccoed front with attic dormers in a Welsh slate mansard roof. The next house has a two storey rubble stone front which probably dates from the 17th century. A third storey of rendered timber-framing with sash windows was added a century later. The left-hand door of no. 17 forms the entrance to no. 16, another house which was probably built in the 17th century but has been re-fronted in brick and cement-rendered. It has a three-light sash window on both the ground and first floor and a sash window in the large gabled attic. No. 15 and the next two houses were said to be 'New built' in c.1699. This property is a two storey rubble stone house with two rendered gables and a stone slate roof. Nos. 13–14 were built as a pair, and they are much grander rubble stone houses, three storeys high with a rendered top floor above a stone band. Each house has a panelled front door with a rectangular fanlight and a small wooden hood.

There is a sudden change of mood at no. 12 where new premises for the Oxford Local Examinations Delegacy (1895–7, T. G. Jackson) were inserted on the site of the Angel's stables. This ashlar stone building has a bold curved gable of Jacobean character and a first floor bow window. Jagged stonework between nos. 12 and 13 indicates unrealized plans for further expansion that would have claimed the older houses to the east. Next, you come to the former History Faculty Library (1954–6, Sir Hubert Worthington), a building of squared rubble stone with a rounded corner and sculpted decoration above the entrance portal. The building was designed before the War, and it occupies the site of Merton Street swimming baths (1869). These indoor baths were a commercial venture, leased by the City for children's swimming lessons from 1924 until 1938 when Cowley Baths were opened. With no. 9 Merton Street, you are back to a three storey ashlar stone house of c.1800. It has a rusticated ground floor, a first floor canted oriel window and a prominent eaves cornice.

Before continuing along Merton Street, it is worth making a short detour up Logic Lane. The intriguing name, first recorded in the mid 17th century, is derived from Aristotle Hall or a school where logicians performed exercises. The sudden kink in the lane marks the former junction with Kybald Street. As we have seen, the eastern section of Kybald Street was closed in 1447; the City began letting the western section to neighbouring colleges in 1567 and Univ purchased the area behind the College in 1851. Beyond the bend, you have a good

10. View north along Logic Lane

view along the stone setts of the lane towards the controversial 1905 bridge. This is all very much part of the College with the Master's Lodgings (1879, G. F. Bodley) to your left and the half-timbered gables of the Durham Building (1903, H. W. Moore) beyond the Goodhart Building (1960–1, Robert Matthew and Marshall-Johnson; major alterations 2015, Freeland Rees Roberts) on your right. The 1960s scheme included the delightful two storey seminar room with a spirelet and weathervane which you can enjoy while returning to Merton Street

You emerge beside the Old Warden's Lodgings for Merton College (1908, Basil Champneys). This stone building is in a free Jacobean style, and has a double bowed front behind an elaborate screen wall; a central gateway and covered staircase lead up to the main door. The height of the building was due to the Warden's insistence on the sun reaching his first floor living rooms! Over-sized as they may be, the Old Warden's Lodgings pale into insignificance beside an unrealized 1878 scheme by T. G. Jackson for a four storey college building which would have extended west from Logic Lane and swallowed up Postmasters' Hall. That scheme became unnecessary when Merton finally assimilated St Alban Hall in 1881, and the College employed Champneys to design St Alban's Quad (1904–10) to replace the old buildings. The street front of St Alban Hall had been re-modelled in about 1860, and Champneys largely retained it, including the Classical doorway (1599) with Tuscan columns and a small semi-circular pediment across the road from Logic Lane. Notice the stone sett crossing to the doorway, offering greater comfort to the daintily-shod. From here, Merton has a continuous frontage which takes us back to the earliest days of the College, although re-facing by Edward Blore (1837–8) erased much interesting detail.

Walter de Merton, later Bishop of Rochester, founded the College in 1264, and soon began acquiring properties here. He purchased three houses east of St John's Church in 1266–8, one of them from Jacob the Jew, and these formed the nucleus of the College while the hall (c. 1274) and other buildings were erected. The original Warden's Lodgings were built on the site of the easternmost house in c.1299–1300, and that stone building with a frontage to Merton Street is recognizable in Loggan's 1675 view; the roof timbers still survive inside the College. The north façade continued with a 15th century range, similar to Blore's work, and the gate-tower which was first conceived in 1418 but only completed in 1465. While re-fronting the gate-tower in 1838, Blore made substantial changes, adding decorated canopies to the statues of Edward I (left) and Walter de Merton (right), and inserting the ornamental central window. He also lowered the sculpture of St John the Baptist (1464–5, Robert Janyns and Son) to a more visible place above the doorway. The sculpture

11. St John the Baptist sculpture, Merton College gateway

12. Glimpse of Merton Real Tennis Court, Merton Street

has been described as summarizing symbolically the major doctrines of the New Testament. You see the saint preaching and the founder of the college kneeling before the Lamb of God and the Book of Seven Seals. Splendid details to look out for include seven different tree species, three birds and hounds chasing rabbits. Beyond the gate-tower, Blore gave a medieval gloss to a short west range added in 1631.

Back on the north side of the street, you can see the Merton Real (Royal) Tennis Court (rebuilt 1798) set back from the road. There were several tennis courts in the city in the 16th and 17th centuries, and this court, the only one still in use, was first recorded in 1595. The lease passed to Thomas Wood, the father of Anthony Wood, in 1610, and it remained in the family until 1754. As noted on a blue plaque beside no. 5 Merton Street, Postmasters' Hall, Anthony Wood (1632–95), the great Oxford historian and antiquary was born, lived and died here. The postmasters or portionists, after whom the house is named, were a class of poor scholars founded by the Merton Fellow, John Wylyot, in c.1380. Each Fellow could elect an eligible scholar who became his servant in return for teaching and 'portions' of food and drink from the hall. The scholars were housed here from c.1507 until 1575, and the property then became a private house. It is a two storey plastered rubble stone building dating from the 16th or 17th century with mullioned windows and two gabled attic dormers in a slate roof. No. 4A next door, the former Merton College stables, was long thought to have medieval origins and detailed investigations in 2006 confirmed that it is indeed one of Oxford's oldest surviving buildings, a stone mansion of c.1200 built for a burgess family called Edrich. The two storey rubble stone building has two blocked windows and

13. Former Merton College stables, 4a Merton Street

a broad gateway on the ground floor; above, two plain stone windows have replaced original windows illustrated in c.1750.

Next comes Beam Hall which takes its name from a former owner, Gilbert de Biham (fl. 1248–54). The building is in two parts, the eastern section having been erected as an academic hall in the late 15th century. It is of rubble stone with original mullioned windows on the ground floor, but the three-light window above the doorway was probably added in c. 1600 when a second storey was added. The stone slate roof has three gabled dormers, the central one being a modern copy. A plaque to the left of the door records that Sir Henry Marten (c.1602–80), M.P., regicide and a graduate of University College was born in the house. Another plaque recalls that Thomas Willis (1621–75), neurologist and Sedleian Professor of Natural Philosophy, lived and worked in the house from 1657 to 1667. The projecting western portion of Beam Hall was built in c.1586, altered in the 18th century and restored by T. G. Jackson in 1885. It is a two storey building with cellars and high gabled attics. The front is cement-faced with imitation masonry joints, a string course above the ground and first floors, and a moulded cornice. Most of the windows are mullioned, and the projecting first floor bay with sash windows replaced a stone mullioned bay existing in 1821. The doorway has a moulded flat wooden bracketed hood. Jackson's restoration of Beam Hall and his New Block (1884–5) next door provided extra accommodation for Corpus Christi College. New Block is a three storey building of Doulting stone, four bays wide with bay windows and gables above a ground floor of semi-circular arches. The building replaced 'The Pit', a stone tenement shown by Loggan in 1675 which led into a yard with houses on every side.

St John the Baptist Church existed by c.1206, and stood on the site of the north range of Merton's Mob Quadrangle. Merton College appropriated this church as its chapel in 1292, but the building also remained a parish church until 1891. The magnificent choir, described by Tyack as 'the finest late 13th century building in Oxford', was built between 1290 and 1294. This was followed by the crossing (c.1330–5) and south transept (1367–8), but halls on the street frontage had to be demolished to make way for the north transept (1416–24). The tower was finally added in 1448–9, but the aisled nave also envisaged by Walter de Merton was never built, and the college chapel plan created here quite by chance became the norm at other Oxford colleges. In 1515, Bishop Fox persuaded Merton to sell him a block of properties west of the College as the site for Corpus Christi College. Merton Grove between the colleges originated as a common way to the city wall 'for a more speedy conveyance therto in times of warr and distraction.' It also provided an outlet for the common sewer which ran down Magpie Lane and gave its name to Gutter Hall in Merton Street. In 1675, Merton had a fives court just west of the chapel, but that area is now an attractively planted garden separated from Merton Street by an early 20th century wrought iron screen and gateway.

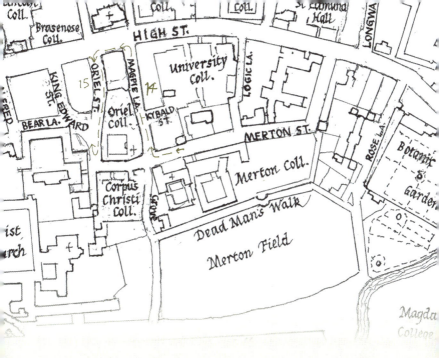

6 Magpie Lane to Oriel Square

As the cobbled surface in Merton Street comes to an end, turn right into Magpie Lane, and head towards High Street with Oriel College Chapel (1637–42) on your left. The street-name plate on the corner tells you that Magpie Lane was formerly Grove Street, a name derived from Merton Grove and current in the 19th century. In c.1230, the street was known as Gropecunt Lane, a name suggesting indecent goings-on that was not uncommon in medieval England! The present name was first used after the former Magpie pub at no. 5 had been licensed in 1657, and it was then reinstated in 1927. On your right, Corpus Christi College added another building (1969, Powell & Moya) beyond New Block which merges neatly around the corner with no. 1 Kybald Street (c.1600), the former Black Lion pub. This is a two storey house of rubble stone and timber-framing with two added gables of c.1630, each of which contains an oriel window supported on brackets. Notice the horizontal sliding sash window and shutters on the ground floor. The first floor has an original stone mullioned window and a late 17th century casement window. A Corpus Fellow, Robert Mowat, probably saved the property in 1931 when he made it his home; his wife claimed credit for restoring a bumble puppy alley, an old pub game like skittles, which they had found derelict in the garden.

Kybald Street, formerly known as Grove or Kybald Place, is the surviving stub of the otherwise lost medieval road that we noted in Logic Lane and Merton Street. It is now an attractive cul-de-sac, closed at the east end by a large pine tree and Grove House. The house is essentially a 17th century three storey roughcast timber-framed building, but the west elevation facing you is later with a boxed-out ground floor with sash windows and an iron first floor balcony. A passageway to the right of the house leads to the Real Tennis Court we saw earlier. Away to the left, a re-sited 17th century stone gateway opens on to Univ's Mitchell Building (1968–71, Architects Design Partnership/John Fryman). Beside it, Kybald House (1887, H.W. Moore) now provides college offices and teaching space but was originally a married tutor's house. It is of brick with stone dressings, shaped gables and a red tiled roof, very much a North Oxford house in the heart of the City.

The former Parsons' Almshouses (1816) occupy the north side of Kybald Street. The building is two storeys high, and of coursed rubble stone with a moulded string course at first floor level and beneath the parapet. Sash windows are hidden behind stone mullioned windows which, like the doorways, are surmounted by hoodmoulds. An inscription panel on the parapet tells us that the building was erected for four old men and four old women following a bequest by Alderman John Parsons (1752–1814). He was founder of the successful Old Bank in High Street at the other end of this property. Occupants of the almshouses had to be over 40, of good reputation, and Anglicans prepared to attend St Mary's Church every Sunday. Men and women were of course accommodated on separate staircases and each person had a front sitting room and a bedroom. A ground floor panel records that the almshouses were acquired by Univ in 1959 and converted into student accommodation following a gift by Helen Altschul, sister of Arthur Goodhart, then Master of the College, and her husband Frank.

While returning to Magpie Lane, notice the grating signed 'J.Lee Iron.Founder' in the gutter opposite the Kybald Street name-plate. James Lee was a brass and iron founder in Oxford in the mid 19th century, with a foundry in Speedwell Street. Opposite the end of Kybald Street, Oriel's medieval rubble stone boundary wall in Magpie Lane is neatly pierced by two oriel windows lighting the Senior Common Room (1971, Oxford Architects' Partnership). Back in Magpie Lane, nos. 6–9 are a row of three storey terraced houses (c.1820) with upper floors of stuccoed timber-framing above a stone ground floor. Each doorcase has a small moulded hood, and the ground floor sash windows have shutters. The taller first floor sashes, lighting the main living rooms, have wooden cornices. Beyond no. 6, a coursed rubble stone wall fronts the former Old Bank stables. Before you reach the gateway, which now leads into the Old Bank Hotel car park, notice a parish boundary stone (1818) in the wall, marking the boundary between the parishes of St John and St Mary the Virgin.

14. St John's parish boundary stone, Magpie Lane

Magpie Lane narrows as you approach High Street, and the rubble stone wall on your left is the east wall of the medieval St Mary Hall which was finally incorporated with Oriel College in 1902. To your right, no. 5 is the former Magpie pub, an early 18th century remodelling of an older house. The three storey front is of roughcast timber-framing; it has a first floor jetty and three gabled attic dormers. The next house, no. 4, is set well back, a roughcast timber-framed house of the 18th century with sash windows on all three floors. No. 3 originated as a two storey house built of coursed rubble stone in the 17th century; two floors of roughcast timber-framing were added a century later. A stone mullioned window on the ground floor survives among the later sashes. The last two houses in Magpie Lane were built on the site of Great and Little Lion Halls. No. 2 dates from c.1623, and it is a three storey roughcast timber-framed house with three gables. The building is jettied out over the narrow street at both floors, and gets most natural light from casement windows in the south elevation. The north elevation has a projecting bay window dated 1613 on the first floor and an eight-light oriel window on the second floor supported by ornamental brackets. No. 1, or Tudor House, is also three storeys high and timber-framed with a roughcast covering. It has a ground floor overhang at the southern end where the supporting beam is dated 1588. The two blocks further north date from the 17th century, and the High Street front was rebuilt in 1902.

You emerge in High Street opposite St Mary the Virgin Church with great views eastwards towards All Souls College and westwards towards Brasenose. Turn left past Oriel's Rhodes Building, and left again into Oriel Street. Effectively bypassed since 1873 by King Edward Street, Oriel Street is an ancient thoroughfare, and probably originated as a roadway inside the Saxon ramparts when Oxford was laid out as a burh in c.900. The southern end of the street beyond today's Oriel Square was blocked by the expansion of St Frideswide's Priory and, later, Corpus Christi College. Oriel Street is first recorded in 1210 as Schidyard Street, a name thought by Anthony Wood to be derived from the makers of shields and scabbards or transcribers of documents. The street was later known as St Mary Hall Lane, and the present name was adopted by 1850.

The external walls of St Mary's Hall Quadrangle dominate the east side of Oriel Street beyond the Rhodes Building. St Mary Hall was established as an academic hall in 1327, leasing the rectory of St Mary the Virgin Church on this site from the newly-founded Oriel College. The hall was always closely linked with Oriel, but it remained a distinct and separate society until it was closed by the University in 1902, the last of the medieval academic halls to be dissolved. The nucleus of the original hall was a building behind six shops in High Street, with a western range in Oriel Street which fell down in c.1446. A stone mullioned window in a rubble stone wall and the entrance gateway to St Mary Hall Quadrangle may be a survival from the subsequent rebuilding. Other buildings around the quad were rebuilt between the 17th and 19th centuries, including the west range in 1825. The Rhodes Building replaced older buildings on the north side of the quad and provided extra accommodation in St Mary's Hall Quadrangle. This was put to unexpected use during the First World War when Somerville College was used as a military hospital and women students and dons were exiled to Oriel. Passages linking St Mary's Hall Quadrangle with the rest of the College were bricked up, but a few hearty male undergraduates tried to break through in June 1919, only to be repelled by a fearless Classics don, Hilda Lorimer, wearing a 'pendant hat with an ostrich feather.'

Traffic-free Oriel Street today can seem almost eerily quiet but, in the early 19th century, coaches heading for the Angel's stables were a regular hazard. Locals nicknamed the coach driver, John Bayzand, 'the sweeper' because he swept carefully into the lane; Bob Taylor was known as 'the scraper' because he cut the corner! Driverless coaches were not unknown and, in January 1828, the horses safely delivered unsuspecting passengers to the Angel after the driver stopped for a drink at the Grapes in Yarnton. Oriel Street was a busy shopping street until the 1870s, and retained shop fronts are a reminder of that era in buildings that now provide student accommodation. Buildings on the west side were built or re-fronted in the early 18th century, and all are at least three storeys high and timber-framed with rendered fronts. The first two houses were built as a single

15. 4 Oriel Street

block between 1713 and 1738 by William Ives, apothecary, and have modern small-paned shop fronts. Ives also erected nos. 3–6 before 1729. Nos. 3–4 have two-light sash windows on the ground floor and 18th century sashes in moulded wooden frames on the upper floors; four steps lead up to the front door of no. 4. The next house was boosted up to five storeys by the later addition of two floors above the cornice. It has a shop front with a modillioned cornice inserted perhaps when the bookseller, William Hayes (d.1822), occupied the premises. Another bookseller, Thomas Boddington, occupied no. 6 between c.1846 and 1866, and he may have added the two semi-circular-headed sash windows enriched with shields which depict the arms of the City and the Diocese of Oxford.

Nos. 7–8 Oriel Street are of one build (c.1720), and the ground floor has a continuous modillioned cornice with two 19th century moulded door frames. The upper floors have sash windows in moulded wood frames, and each house has a large attic dormer with a six-light casement window. Both properties were named Carter House after restoration in 1984 in honour of Jimmy Carter, President of the United States of America from 1977 to 1981.

Nos. 9 and 10 were built as one house between 1724 and 1738, and have a modern 18th or 19th century style shop front. There are sash windows in the upper floors and two attic gables, each with a modern casement window. Between no. 10 and 11, a passageway provides a tantalizing glimpse of the rubble stone walled Harris Lecture Theatre. This is the former Oriel tennis court, first recorded in 1577, and played in during the Civil War by Charles I and Prince Rupert. Edward, Prince of Wales, the future Edward VII, played tennis here in 1859, but the building was also used as a temporary theatre and a billiard room during the 19th century; by 1923, Oriel was using it as a lecture theatre. The front part of no.12 Oriel Street was rebuilt in the early 18th century, perhaps as two houses, and it is three storeys high with a central chimney stack between two gables. An interesting early 17th century rubble stone and timber-framed back wing was retained, approached by a side passage. Two modern sash windows on the ground floor replaced a shop front at no. 12, and shop fronts were also removed from the last two properties, formerly nos. 14 and 15, when they were incorporated into the adjacent neo-Classical building in Oriel Square (1951, Russell Cox). On the other side of Oriel Street, beyond the side elevation of the College Library (1788, James Wyatt), a rubble stone wall with a dressed coping forms the boundary until you reach the Carter Building (1729) on the west side of the Back Quadrangle.

Oriel Square may seem to have changed little over the centuries, but the road layout was formerly very different, and the present name was only officially adopted in 1953. In the medieval period, Oriel Street continued south past Merton Street to St Frideswide's Priory, but the President's Lodgings for Corpus Christi College built in 1599 blocked this route. Two roads branched off westwards from Oriel Street, the modern Bear Lane and Shitbourne Lane, a lost street south of and parallel to Bear Lane which joined a continuation of today's Alfred Street. The name Shitbourne suggests a watercourse filled with sewage so the closure of the lane by 1397 was perhaps not unwelcome. The junction of Oriel Street with Bear Lane had to be altered when King Edward Street was built in 1873. The new street disgorged traffic into a confused area, exposing to view the Provost of Oriel's stables opposite the college gateway and the rear elevation of Christ Church's Peckwater Quadrangle (1706–14, Henry Aldrich). Oriel College, Christ Church and the Oxford Local Board collaborated on an improvement scheme which saw the stables cleared away, and the road set back to its present width. Paved with granite setts, the area became a convenient cab rank with a cabmen's shelter like the one which survives in St Giles'.

The new public space provided enhanced views of Christ Church's monumental Canterbury Gate (1775–8, James Wyatt), Corpus Christi College (c.1514–17; second floor added, 1737) and, especially, the Oriel College west range (1620–2). The last is of ashlar stone and three storeys high with a cresting of little shaped gables; the central gate tower is slightly taller with an embattled parapet and a first-floor oriel window, repeating the architectural feature which had given the college its nickname. Through the gateway you get a glimpse of the porch (rebuilt 1897) leading into the hall and niches above containing statues of Edward I, James I and the Virgin and Child. On the west side of the street, Christ Church built an ornamental wall and screen (1877–9, Bodley and Garner) between Bear Lane and Canterbury Quad to improve the area behind Peckwater Quad which now accommodated a college wash-house. To the north, however, the side elevations of properties in King Edward Street and Oriel Street presented a visual hotch-potch until Oriel filled this gap in the early 1950s, and created today's square.

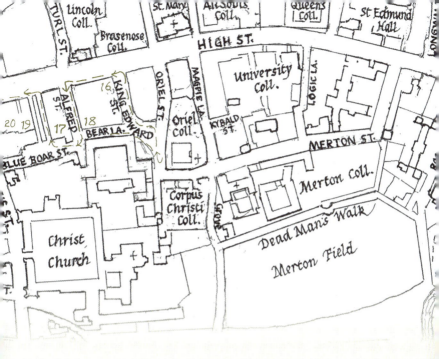

7 Bear Lane to Blue Lamp Alley

As you leave Oriel Square, walk a few paces along Bear Lane in the deep shadow cast by Peckwater Quad. No. 5 is a three storey 17th century house of roughcast timber-framing with a first floor jetty; each floor has a sash window. The next house dates from the 19th century, and has a two storey stuccoed front with sash windows, a cornice and a parapet masking the roof. Quartermaine's Stables (c.1835) are of red brick with a central elliptical arch inscribed with the name. The façade was retained when derelict stables at the back were redeveloped to form new courtyard accommodation for Lincoln College (1978, Oxford Architects' Partnership/Geoffrey Beard). No. 7 Bear Lane was retained as part of that scheme, and is a three storey house of roughcast timber-framing dating from the 18th or 19th century. Now retrace your steps to King Edward Street, and head towards High Street. Outside no. 11, Peckwater House, notice a grey painted electricity sub-station signed 'Lucy Oxford', a later product by the foundry which supplied so much of the city's public ironwork. Next door, no. 12 was the childhood home of Ivy Williams (1877–1966), the first woman barrister in England in 1922, and a generous benefactor to Oxford Town and Gown. Almost opposite at no. 6, an elaborate plaque with a bust of Cecil

16. Carved head, Shepherd & Woodward shopfront, 109 High Street

Rhodes records that the already wealthy diamond mining entrepreneur kept 'academical residence' there in 1881 while studying at Oriel.

The discreet entrance to the Vincent Club, a club for elite sportsmen and women established at no. 90 High Street in 1863, is at no. 1a. Business premises on the prestigious corner of High Street justified higher expenditure, and Shepherd and Woodward's shop front at no. 109 has some carved stone heads. No. 108 (1873, Frederick Codd), on the opposite corner, was more elaborately decorated for Hitchcock and Sons, chemists. A series of carvings by Samuel Grafton, Oxford sculptor, represent the heads of sovereigns, particularly Edward II, titular founder of Oriel College in 1326, and other College benefactors. Two doors further along, at no. 106–7, it is worth asking inside for permission to view the medieval remains of Tackley's Inn, the first home of Oriel College in the 1320s. Part of the south wall of the early 14th century academic hall survives, complete with a Y-tracery two-light window, and you can also see two bays of the 15th century collar-beam hall roof. The early 14th century rib-vaulted cellar provided a storage area below the shops in the front part of the building, and has been described as 'the best preserved of the medieval cellars in the city.'

Now walk along High Street towards Carfax, enjoying the exquisite decorative carving on the Brasenose College front (1887–1911, T. G. Jackson). Turn left beyond The Ivy Restaurant into narrow Alfred Street which retains a road surface of granite slabs and setts. The street is announced by an early cast-iron street name plate (c.1840) above the shop front opposite. Until the foundation of Cardinal

17. St Columba's Church, Alfred Street

College in 1525, the street continued south beyond the present Bear Lane to Frideswide Lane north of the priory. On your left, beyond the Victorian bank building, the unlovely 1960s extension displays the arms of the pre-merger Westminster Bank.

Across the road, no. 3 Alfred Street retains a stuccoed ground floor of c.1800, but the upper floors were rebuilt in the 1960s. The round-headed front door led originally to the rooms where the pioneering physical educationist, Archibald Maclaren (d.1894), opened a gymnasium in the 1840s, and taught undergraduates such as William Morris and Edward Burne-Jones to fence.

No. 4 is a chequer brick three storey house with black painted lintels (c.1840) which incorporates an ashlar stone pier from the original frontage of St Columba's Church (1914, T. Phillips Figgis; re-fronted 1960, E. Brian Smith). The church was built for Presbyterian members of the University on the site of the Bear Inn stables, which the Mitre had taken over in the early 19th century. The local historian, Henry Minn, noted sadly that, before giving up the stables, the Mitre 'made a bonfire of all the old books and ledgers in the yard.' When the present four storey Georgian-style building was erected in the 1960s, archaeologists excavated footings and burials from St Edward's Church. The

18. Former Oxford Gymnasium, Alfred Street

church was first recorded in 1122, and the parish was united with neighbouring St Frideswide's parish in 1298. This combined parish was still very small, however, and the church probably closed by 1388. The Bear pub on the corner of Blue Boar Street also occupies part of the site of the church. It is a timber-framed building and probably 17th century in origin, but the three storey front is stuccoed with casement windows and a single horizontal sliding sash window on the upper floors. During the 18th century, the pub was known as the Jolly Trooper, and it only assumed the present name after the Bear Inn in High Street closed in 1801. The cosy pub interior is famous for its collection of ties begun in 1952 by Alan Course, a previous landlord.

On the opposite corner, Blue Boar Court was built as the Oxford Gymnasium (1859, William Wilkinson) for Archibald Maclaren, and demonstrates the contemporary success of his business. It is a two storey building of yellow brick which is considered to be the finest example of Ruskin's Italian Gothic style in Oxford. Long rows of lofty sash windows provided ventilation in summer, and, in bad weather, windows in the roof lantern served the same purpose. The interior provided space for physical training, gymnastics, boxing and fencing, and the large central area open to the roof made possible high climbing and swinging exercises. Holywell Press Ltd., established at no. 47 Holywell Street in c.1899, moved into the building in 1920, but Oxford University Boxing Club was still based here until the Second World War. Holywell Press converted the premises into offices in 1989 and they were refurbished in 2014. Maclaren built an extension in Alfred Street (1861, William Wilkinson) for children and delicate pupils, but this was demolished in the 1960s. In the years before 1914, the building served as the headquarters of Oxford University Officers' Training Corps and, after the outbreak of war, hundreds of graduates who had undergone preliminary training during their degree courses queued along the street to be interviewed for commissions as junior officers.

Alfred Street today is brought to an abrupt halt by a rubble stone wall and the backs of Christ Church's Peckwater Quadrangle. Cardinal College and Christ Church acquired and reshaped much of the former Great Jewry after 1525, extinguishing the network of streets between St Aldate's and Oriel Street. Bear Lane survived as it defined the northern boundary of Christ Church, but Civil School or Jury Lane further south, which linked Alfred Street with St Aldate's, now ran through college property. In 1553, the Sub-Dean of Christ Church, Dr Tresham, purchased from Edward Frere part of the site of St Edward's Hall, south of the present Bear pub, and created what we know as Blue Boar Street. Frere, the owner of the Blackfriars site in St Ebbe's, agreed to supply stone from there to build the rubble wall on the south side of the street which still exists. The new road was initially known as Tresham's Lane or New Lane but, by the mid 17th century, it was commonly named after the Blue Boar Inn at the St Aldate's end. The rubble stone wall is now over topped by the Blue Boar Quadrangle (1968, Powell & Moya) which replaced former college stables and the remains of another indoor tennis court. Boffin's had a large bakery on the north side of Blue Boar Street in 1897, and several older buildings remained in the 1930s, but the site is largely now a seating area between the Bear and Ebor House, the ashlar stone-fronted former Chief Constable's house (1896). The latter was a cut-price job by the City Estates Surveyor after the City rejected a more elaborate scheme by Henry Hare, architect of the Town Hall.

Now make your way through the seating area, and walk into Wheatsheaf Yard, rebuilt in 1898 as part of the redevelopment of nos. 127–9 High Street. The red brick Wheatsheaf on the left replaced an earlier pub of the same name; the first pub on the site was the Hen and Chickens, licensed in 1662. To your right, a glance through the window will make clear that Oxford Nails offers a quite different service from Gill & Co., the ironmongers which had a shop here from c.1953 until 2010. Gill's claimed to date from 1530, making it one of the oldest businesses in the country but the Gill family only became involved in c.1840.

19. Chiang–Mai Restaurant, 130a High Street

Emerging into High Street, turn left and left again down a passageway to see no. 130a High Street, now the Chiang-Mai restaurant. This is a remarkable building, erected behind his house by Alderman William Boswell (d.1638) in 1637 – notice the date above the wood-framed doorway. You would expect to find a low-quality house on this restricted backland site, but the property reflects both Boswell's personal wealth and the high value of city centre land at the time. Usually called Kemp Hall from an earlier academic hall on the site, the house is a largely timber-framed structure, apart from a stone plinth and the stone back wall containing the chimney stacks. It is of two storeys with cellars and five attic gables, and the east elevation is jettied at first and second floor levels. Natural light is admitted by a rich profusion of windows, including five bracketed oriels on the first floor and mullioned windows in the gables. Inside, the building retains the original main staircase, as well as fireplaces and doorways. Between

1870 and 1895, Kemp Hall improbably served as the City Police Station, and the passageway leading to it became known as Blue Lamp Alley because of the lamp at the High Street entrance. The cells were in a smaller gabled building to the south which was dated 1611 on the decorative plasterwork. That property was demolished for the new Town Hall in c.1893, but Kemp Hall survived and was carefully restored (1929, William Daft) to become a café; it has been an eating house ever since.

Return to High Street and investigate the next alleyway beneath Payne & Son's mastiff, which leads to no. 131a, the Chequers Inn. Notice on your right some original 15th century studding, and the remains of two original timber doorways, one with roses on the lintel. Facing you as you enter the yard, there is an original 17th century three-light Ipswich window with an arched middle light. The Chequers was probably built by Alderman Richard Kent in c.1500 when it was known as Kent's Hall. It consists of a three storey east-facing range which is now masked by a modern balcony and an external staircase. Beyond this range, there is a 17th century two storey extension and, across the yard, a two storey building of coursed rubble stone that formed the inn's kitchen. A piece of elaborate 15th century stone panelling set into the north wall of the bar provides the best possible excuse to go inside and enjoy a drink before walking the last few paces to Carfax.

20. 15th century stone panelling, bar of Chequers Inn, 131a High Street

8 Botanic Garden to Rose Lane

The walk begins in a tranquil spot beside the river Cherwell between the Botanic Garden and the south-west corner of Magdalen Bridge (1772–9, John Gwynn). You can really appreciate the scale of the structure from here as it crosses two major river channels and the intervening island on a series of arches. In summer, you should be able to see people manoeuvring their punts and pedaloes on the Cherwell as well as passing buses and pedestrians on the roadway above. Three large semi-circular arches carry the roadway over this western channel of the river which was widened and deepened in the 1770s to reduce the incidence of flooding. Notice the sculpted head of a bearded man over the central arch, and the head of the goddess Isis over the blocked towpath archway. A plaque above the left-hand arch records that the foundation stone of the bridge was laid on March 26th, 1773, and that Oxford Local Board widened the bridge and rebuilt the parapets in 1882–3. A circular plaque marks the successful completion of the Oxford Preservation Trust fund-raising campaign (1989–93), which enabled Oxfordshire County Council to renew decayed cast concrete balusters in natural stone.

Downstream, beyond an old ashlar

21. Sculpted head of goddess Isis, Magdalen Bridge

stone boundary wall with a vase finial, you have tantalising glimpses of Botanic Garden greenhouses and walks beside the Cherwell. Heading away from the river, you see Magdalen Tower rising majestically above the bridge parapet. This south-west corner of the bridge was only completed in 1790, having been long delayed by the University's reluctance to allow the demolition of the Professor of Botany's house and library on the site. The Professor's house had been created in the early 18th century by adding a second storey to a long south-facing 'winter house for plants' that was probably built in 1670–1. The library was re-housed in a converted orangery within the Botanic Garden (1789, James Wyatt) and, after Charles Daubeny became Professor of Botany in 1834, that building was further adapted (1835, H. J. Underwood) to become the Professor's house with a stuccoed five bay Grecian front and four Ionic columns facing High Street; it now provides graduate accommodation for Magdalen College.

As you walk along here, you are slightly below the level of High Street which was raised at this point in the 1770s to provide a gradual approach to Magdalen Bridge. Until then, there was level access from the street to the Oxford Botanic Garden, the first physic garden in England, founded in 1621. The founder, Henry Danvers, first Earl of Danby (1573–1644), was a retired military man who may have been inspired by the Jardin des Plantes in Paris while serving in France. Another possibility is that he was something of a hypochondriac and was persuaded to take up the project by his doctor, Sir Thomas Clayton, Regius Professor of Medicine. Whatever his motives, Danby leased from Magdalen College five acres of low-lying meadowland in Paris Mead. The site included the former burial ground of the Jewish community in Oxford which St John's Hospital had continued to use until 1457. The University's scavenger raised the land with 4,000 loads of 'mucke and dunge' to counteract flooding and high ashlar stone boundary walls were built around the site. The Danby Gateway (1632, Nicholas Stone) was built in the northern wall to serve as the main entrance and it is an imposing two storey Classical structure of Headington stone. Niches either side of the archway contain later, now decayed, statues of Charles I and Charles II, partly paid for, according to tradition, by a fine imposed on Anthony Wood for intemperate words against the Earl of Clarendon! In the main pediment above the archway, there is a bust of Danby himself (1695, John Vanderstein).

A glimpse of the central fountain and sunlit paths through the archway will probably tempt you into visiting the Botanic Garden (admission charge), which you enter through a small gateway to the left of the Danby Gate. Emerging from the visitor centre, you may like to spend a few moments considering the history of the garden, perhaps from the comfort of a nearby bench. The walls and gateways around the garden were complete by 1633, but it was only in 1639–40 that 'outlandish workmen', presumably foreigners, laid out the Walled Garden following a plan by Jacob Bobart (c.1599–1679), a German from Brunswick. He had been appointed as the first Hortus Praefectus or superintendent of the garden at an annual salary of £40 'in consideration of his dressing, manuring and planting the sayed garden.' He was described as a 'prince of plants' and he was also a great eccentric who tagged his long beard with silver thread on feast days and went for walks with a pet goat. His son, also Jacob (d.1719), went on to become Professor of Botany in 1683. The Oxford ragwort which he imported from Sicily in c.1700 soon escaped from the garden and it spread with the railway network in the 19th century to become common across the country. Zacharias von Uffenbach, a German visitor to the Physic Garden in 1710, described the younger Bobart as 'a good horticulturalist' but of an evil appearance that was exceeded only by his wife's.

Key figures in the later history of the garden included the great botanist and plant collector, Dr William Sherard (d. 1726), who presented his herbarium to the University, and endowed the professorship which still bears his name. The first post holder was John James Dillenius (1684-1747), a celebrated German botanist, who welcomed Carl Linnaeus to the Physic Garden in 1736. Dillenius is said to have disapproved at first of Linnaeus's system for classifying plants, but he was convinced after the young Swedish naturalist described the structure of ivy-leaved toadflax, a plant still common on walls in and around the garden. Notable later professors have included Dr John Sibthorp (1758–96) who left his library of natural history and his drawings to the Physic Garden and Charles Daubeny (d.1868). The latter was responsible for many improvements to the garden and changed its name to the Oxford Botanic Garden in 1840. He delighted William Baxter, the Scottish gardener, by adopting plans to raise and level low-lying areas that had been impossible to cultivate because of frequent flooding. Daubeny was well-known for his garden parties, one of which he held for victorious Darwinians after the famous Oxford debate between Huxley and Wilberforce in 1860. On these occasions, he would show visitors the monkeys that he kept in cages fixed to the Danby Gate.

Bobart's original Walled Garden was divided into quarters by two straight walks which intersected in the middle. The walks were bounded by yew hedges on both sides, and 18th century visitors were requested not to 'break through, or leap over the Hedges and Fences in the garden'. Anyone wishing to view the plants within the quarters had to be attended by the professor or the gardener. The well-tended garden rather improbably became the launch site for James Sadler's first public balloon ascent on November 12th, 1784, and perhaps for his very first flight on October 4th. This must have been with the blessing of Dr John Sibthorp who had allowed Sadler to launch a trial balloon from his new house in Cowley Place in February 1784.

By 1834, the yew hedges beside the walks had all gone, and the quarters were sub-divided by two north-south walks, named Dog Walk and Boar Walk after sculptures copied from originals in the Uffizi Gallery in Florence. The boar eventually disintegrated, but the dog was re-housed to Fisher Row behind the University Surveyor's Offices in the 1960s and can now be seen at the Old Malthouse in Tidmarsh Lane. The garden's original quarters were subsequently reinstated, and the junction of the main walks, where Sadler's hazardous flights began, is adorned with a 19th century circular pond with a stone basin surmounted by a central basin and fountain. One Victorian professor is said to have fallen into this fountain while learning to ride his penny-farthing bicycle.

Most visitors to the Botanic Garden come to see the plants, but the evolution of the buildings is also intriguing. To replace the first orangery that backed on to High Street, William Townesend built two single storey orangeries against the north wall of the garden in 1733–5, which were heavily rusticated to match the Danby Gate. Both have since been modified and incorporated within later buildings. The orangery east of the Danby Gate was first adapted in 1789, as we have seen, and then further modified in 1835 by H. J. Underwood. Underwood's identical plan for Townesend's orangery west of the Danby Gate was not realised, but a second storey was added to the building in 1848 to create the Daubeny Laboratory. This is a two storey ashlar stone building with a moulded first floor cornice and a parapet with a moulded cornice below it; rectangular rusticated panels at first floor level echo Townesend's original design. The Manley Laboratory (1902, A. Mardon Mowbray) to the west of the Daubeny Laboratory and the Vines Wing (1910–12) to the east also remained faithful to Townesend's work, and all these buildings, now known as West Block, provide a fine architectural backdrop to the garden. The first glasshouses in the Botanic Garden were wooden lean-to structures built either side of the Danby Gate in c.1734 which survived until the mid-19th century.

Walking to the far end of West Block, you come to a 19th century copy of the Warwick Vase which Daubeny probably purchased for the Botanic Garden in the 1830s. The original had been found at Hadrian's Villa in Tivoli near Rome in the 18th century and was long displayed at Warwick Castle. Heading south beside the garden wall, you pass the small western gateway (1632, Nicholas Stone) which bears the founder's name and the date in Roman numerals. Further along, you reach the 1648 bed, planted below the southern garden wall. This features some of the 1,600 plants included in the first catalogue of the Physic Garden published that year. The catalogue demonstrated Bobart's remarkable success in creating a new garden from scratch in a few years – years that had been dominated by the English Civil War (1642–6). At the junction of the southern and central walks, you will find a yew tree planted during that conflict in 1645, the oldest living plant in the Botanic Garden.

Loggan's view of the Physic Garden in 1675 shows a narrow strip of cultivated garden outside the walled garden, accessible through the eastern gateway (1632–3, Nicholas Stone) and a small gate in the southern garden wall. The latter had been widened by the 1730s to create the opening that exists today. In 1947, the Botanic Garden realised a long-held ambition by expanding further south into part of Christ Church Meadow that had latterly been used as war-time allotments. You can begin to explore the delightful Lower Garden by dawdling past the oval pond and rock garden before turning right towards the autumn border. Behind a tall wooden fence, notice The Cottage (private), a picturesque house for the superintendent or curator of the Botanic Garden. The back wall of The Cottage may date back to Bobart's time (c.1640), but the present building is essentially a two storey double-fronted house of ashlar stone which probably dates from the 18th century. It has a stone slate roof and two gables of unequal size, one with a sash window and the other with a casement.

Continuing along the path beside the autumn border, you come to the water garden next to the river Cherwell. The Bacchic Vase, decorated with pan pipes and grapes and provided with goats' heads for handles, forms a striking architectural feature. Like the Warwick Vase we saw earlier, this is a 19th century copy of an ancient vase and again probably purchased by Daubeny. Having savoured the view back towards the Walled Garden and Magdalen Tower, you can enjoy a riverside walk which will eventually bring you to Magdalen Bridge. The delights of the Lower Garden are a distraction at any season, but you also have a splendid panorama across the Cherwell and Magdalen College School playing field towards St Hilda's College. St Hilda's – a women's college until 2008 – was founded in 1893 in Cowley House (c.1780), which Dr John Sibthorp had built to replace the soon to be demolished Professor's house next to Magdalen Bridge. This can be distinguished as a three storey brick building three bays wide with a central white painted bay window and two ground floor Venetian windows. A red and yellow brick Gothic range (1862, Deane & Woodward) had already been added to the north, and St Hilda's made further extensions, both to the south (1897, P. Day and 1909, W. E. Mills) and to the north (1934, Sir Edwin Cooper). The latest addition to the south (2018–20, Gort Scott) features a prominent tower and a riverside pavilion among buildings designed to provide the College with a new 'front door' on Cowley Place. Beyond them, you can see the green copper roof of a Magdalen College School teaching block (2006, Buttress Fuller Alsop Williams). Further south, to the right of the school sports' pavilion, yellow brick Cherwell Edge (1877–8, William Wilkinson) was built as a private house for the Vernon Harcourt family, and became a teachers' training college by 1897. St Hilda's acquired the building in 1921, and added a new range to the north (1925, N.W. Harrison).

Back in the Botanic Garden, you will be approaching the glasshouses outside the eastern garden wall. Daubeny first sited them here in 1851, and the superstructures have been replaced several times, most recently in 1971. You will almost certainly want to visit the Arid House, the Palm House, the Insectivorous House and the Lily House before resuming the walk towards Magdalen Bridge. Punts and pedaloes on the river make for a lively scene in summer, but the view here is always Oxford at its most

22. Bacchic Vase, Botanic Garden

beguiling. Notice the unexpectedly grand scale of the south elevation of Magdalen Bridge which consists of a long causeway between arched bridges over the two branches of the river Cherwell. Look out also for the white-painted Chinese style timber bridges which delightfully provide Magdalen College School with access to its riverside meadows.

Leaving the Botanic Garden, you will find a plaque (1931) on the west elevation of the Danby Gate recording the former Jewish burial place in this area. Another Jewish memorial plaque has been placed beside the steps leading up to the Penicillin Memorial Rose Garden (1953, Dame Sylvia Crowe). An inscribed stone records that the garden was presented by the Albert and Mary Lasker Foundation of New York 'in honour of the research workers in this university who discovered the clinical importance of penicillin for saving of life, relief of suffering and inspiration to future research.' The Rose Garden occupies the site of the Noah's Ark pub and adjoining buildings which were demolished to widen the High Street in the 1790s. Walking through the garden is always a pleasure, but you also have fine views of Magdalen Tower and of the north elevations of the Botanic Garden West Block. Note the appropriate Latin inscription 'Sine experientia nihil sufficienter sciri potest' (Without experiment nothing can be sufficiently known) above the door of the Manley Laboratory. This scene would look very different today if Sir Henry Tizard, President of Magdalen College, had persuaded the College Governing Body to accept Oliver Hill's ambitious 1948 scheme to build new ranges either side of the Danby Gate.

You emerge into Rose Lane opposite the three storey east elevation of no. 61 High Street (1802), and its former service wing, now no. 1 Rose Lane. The latter is also of ashlar stone and three storeys high, but very much lower and plainer than the main house. Rose Lane has been so-called since the mid 18th century, probably because of flowers grown in market gardens on the site of Merton's Garden Buildings. Previously, it had been Trinity Lane, recalling the Trinitarian Friars whose house lay on the west side of the street in the 14th century. The lane was formed in c.1200 to provide a convenient link between High Street and the grange, or farm, of St Frideswide's Priory, and there seems to have been a gate at the High Street end. A conduit carrying water from Holywell to Merton College by way of St John's Hospital was authorised in 1267 and, as late as 1675, a stream still ran along the west side of the lane before deviating to the right and passing below the city wall. By that time, Merton College land between the lane and the city wall was clearly being cultivated as a market garden, and members of the Bates family ran a nursery there from 1782 until the 1930s.

Since the 1620s, the high stone wall and western gateway of the Physic Garden has dominated the other side of the lane, and a few tall trees, including a chile pine or monkey puzzle, are survivors from a scheme by Professor Daubeny in the 1850s to create a pinetum on this strip of land. Rose Lane briefly became busy during the 1770s when it formed part of the temporary road between High Street and St Clement's while Magdalen Bridge was being rebuilt. Peace was restored once traffic started using the new bridge in 1778, and the lane was little disturbed until 1839 when St Peter in the East parish school was built at the far end, beyond the nursery. This school had as many as 117 children in 1866 but, with the gradual depopulation of central Oxford, it closed in 1929. Merton College's Garden Buildings (1939–40, Sir Hubert Worthington) occupied the sites of both the school and the nursery. This development was said to have transformed the lane into 'one of the most charming roads in Oxford,' replacing the high nursery wall by a long, low structure with projecting wings in a green setting. Attic rooms were added to the original two storey rubble stone building in 1989, and the T. S. Eliot Lecture Theatre (2010, Ridge) in the south-west corner recalls the poet's association with Merton College.

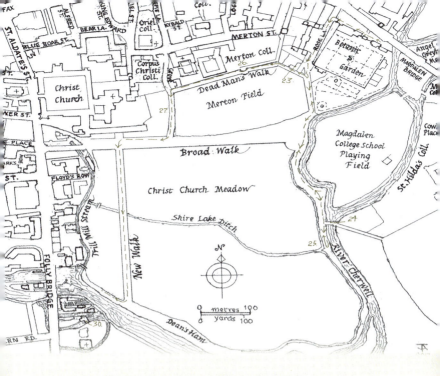

9 Christ Church Meadow

You have now reached the entrance to Christ Church Meadow, a precious piece of countryside in the heart of Oxford. If Cyril Jackson, Dean of Christ Church, had had his way in 1803, you would be entering the meadow through a magnificent stone gateway designed by the architect, G. Smith. Instead, you have to wriggle through the pedestrian entrance in a 19th century screen of tall cast-iron spears which was a later more modest option. The public has long enjoyed free access to Christ Church Meadow, but admission is still essentially regulated by bylaws issued in 1867, and you can see an updated version on a discreet grey notice beneath the huge plane tree to your left. Large wooden boards at the various entrances used to trumpet more forcefully the host of objectionable activities, including 'the flying of kites, throwing stones, throwing balls, bowling hoops, shooting arrows, firing guns or pistols' which may still today lead to expulsion by the college meadow-keepers. The Revd W. E. Sherwood recalled that the only hoop he saw in the Broad Walk belonged to the Dean's youngest daughter; 'All children of less illustrious descent ... had to be "under control" like the dogs under a rabies order.' To your right, you will already have noticed Meadow Cottages, a picturesque

23. Meadow Cottages, Rose Lane

pair of two storey rubble stone cottages with four red tile hung gables and a red tile roof. The cottages retain some ancient mullioned windows, and probably date from the 17th century, but they have been restored and altered. They occupy part of the site of the grange or farm belonging to St Frideswide's Priory just outside the south-east corner of the city wall. Beyond the cottages, you have sudden spectacular views across Merton Field towards the Broad Walk and along the line of the city wall to Merton College and Christ Church.

How has this landscape evolved over the centuries? Christ Church Meadow is actually a group of meadows that became united under the ownership of Christ Church. They include Merton Field, Priesthey (the area south of the Broad Walk), Stockwell Mead (the area nearest the Thames) and Earl's Ham (the boathouse island). These low-lying meadows are or were separated from each other by branches of the Cherwell or the Thames which have, in some cases, become mere shadows of their former selves, or have simply disappeared. Shire Lake, today an easily missed ditch running from west to east across Christ Church Meadow between Priesthey and Stockwell Mead, was a significant enough branch of the Thames to become the boundary between Oxfordshire and Berkshire in the 11th century. An early river channel along the northern edge of Christ Church Meadow from the Cherwell to Trill Mill Stream may have been robbed of water by the building of mill streams before its remains were lost beneath the Broad Walk.

St Frideswide's Priory had acquired the meadows north of Shire Lake by the mid 12th century, and constructed the grange from which the priory's fields in Cowley parish could be cultivated. Rose Lane provided one link between the two, but the canons of St Frideswide's may also have built Milham Bridge across the Cherwell as an alternative route in c.1300. This bridge was in fact two bridges and a causeway, and its western end was at what is now the south-west tip of the Botanic Garden. Milham Bridge was rebuilt by Cardinal Wolsey in 1525 as a means of bringing building materials to his new college, and Merton Field perhaps acquired the alternative name Timber Yard because carpenters worked there on that grand project. Once Christ Church was completed, the bridge continued to be used as a horse- and footway until part of it collapsed in 1634. The rest was demolished during the Civil War and Christ Church chose not to rebuild the bridge because 'it would make their College and Merton a Thoroughfare for Country People on Market Days, who sometimes would drive their smaller sort of Cattle through their Quads to the great Disturbance of Students'. Anthony Wood also noted that the bridge had been much frequented at night by scholars and townsmen wishing to commit robberies in nearby villages! As we have seen, the Milham route was temporarily re-instated with timber bridges between 1772 and 1778 during the rebuilding of Magdalen Bridge, but it was subsequently abandoned. Frederick King recalled that, during the 1830s, Milham Ford, over the eastern channel of the Cherwell, was still well used during hay harvest to access the meadow which is now Magdalen College School playing field.

Near Milham Bridge, and beside the Cherwell, St Frideswide's Priory established a hermitage which became known as Our Lady in the Wall because of effigies of the Virgin Mary on the adjoining oratory. The hermit living there may have had some responsibility for maintaining the bridge. People at the nearby grange looked after him, and also entertained pilgrims to St Edmund's Well in St Clement's. The oratory became a focus for prayer and Anthony Wood recounts the story of a poor student who prayed so often and so pitiably that the Virgin Mary appeared to him and sent him off to Thomas Becket, Archbishop of Canterbury, with the promise of a newly vacant rectory. The hermitage ended its days as a tool store for workmen working on Cardinal College and no trace of it survives.

The low-lying meadows and river channels south of the city wall effectively formed part of Oxford's defences in medieval times and, during the Civil War, a cut was made from the river Cherwell in 1643 so that Christ Church Meadow could swiftly be flooded in the event of a siege. The old city wall in front of Merton College was strengthened, and a cannon was mounted on the bastion

24. Jubilee Bridge over river Cherwell

which still provides a fine view from the Fellows' Garden. In 1644–5, an outer line of earthworks was constructed in Christ Church Meadow, running from east to west along the line of the Broad Walk and then south to the river Thames between today's New Walk and Trill Mill Stream. At this end, beside the Cherwell, there was a bastion (Half Moon Sconce) bisected by the river and the earthwork then continued along the opposite bank towards Magdalen Bridge. These defences were destroyed soon after the Civil War, but, with the eye of faith, you can conjure up the line of the bastion in the path which heads south from the Broad Walk around the eastern boundary of the meadow. You may wish to follow this path for some way to see, and enjoy the view from, the Jubilee Bridge (2014). This bridge replaced a hand-operated ferry that took Christ Church students across the Cherwell to the college sports field opened in the 1860s. A little further on, you come to the eastern end of Shire Lake, the former county boundary, from which there are lovely views across the meadow towards Christ Church.

You can of course continue around Christ Church Meadow to Folly Bridge from here but, in order to enjoy Dead Man's Walk and other delights, you need to retrace your steps to Meadow Cottages just inside the Rose Lane gate. On the way, as you are walking through the trees at the end of the Broad Walk, notice a raised concrete structure on your left. This marks the beginning of Oxford's main outfall sewer, built after long debate in the 1870s, and reconstructed a century later. When you reach the cottages, turn

25. Eastern end of Shire Lake ditch

left along the path which leads to the city wall below Merton College. Almost at once, you will see on your right a plaque commemorating James Sadler's first balloon flight 'from near this place' on October 4th, 1784. The exact launch site is unknown but, as we have seen, it was probably in the Physic Garden. Beyond a single storey stone cottage with a brick side elevation, you join the city wall at the south-east corner of the medieval defences. You are now in Dead Man's Walk, by tradition the route outside the walls taken by funeral processions from the Jewry in St Aldate's to the Jewish burial ground until 1290. Another theory is that the name recalls Colonel Francis Windebank who may have been shot here, rather than at the Castle, in April 1645 after he was court-martialled for surrendering Bletchingdon House, a Royalist stronghold, to Oliver Cromwell without a struggle. In fact, this walk below the city wall seems not to have existed before the 18th century and John Walker records that the sunny south-

26. Bastion and city wall along Dead Man's Walk

facing wall was 'commonly called the Dead-man's Wall from being so warm as to revive a man almost dead with cold'. From Dead Man's Wall to Dead Man's Walk was a simple step. You pass the cut-down bastion where a Civil War cannon was mounted, and soon reach Merton College Fellows' Quadrangle (1608–10, John Acroyd of Halifax). Tyack has described this as 'the first large-scale extension to a medieval Oxford college', and other colleges followed Merton's lead in the years leading up to the Civil War as they sought to house growing numbers of students. It was Oxford's first three storey college quad, and it has a symmetrical south elevation to the meadow with oriel windows in the end bays and a central doorway. It was built of local Headington stone by Yorkshire building workers who not only under-cut local men but also perhaps brought skills lacking in a city where there had been few major projects for 80 years.

Fellows' Quad was known as Great Quad until the late 19th century to distinguish it from Little or Mob Quad. Initially, the building would have been partially hidden by the city wall but, during the 18th century, Merton College obtained the City's permission to lower the old wall and install the decorative iron railings topped by gilded pine-cones which are such a feature today. A few paces further along the path, and through the railings, you have a fine view of the south and west ranges of Mob Quadrangle (1371–8, William Humbervyle) and the Chapel tower (1448–51) behind them. These two ranges completed the oldest quadrangle in Oxford, and they contained a college library – again Oxford's oldest – above ground floor rooms. They were built of rubble stone from Wheatley and dressed stone from Taynton near Burford, and roofed with Cotswold stone slates. Why Mob Quad? The name is first recorded in 1797, and may refer to the fact that junior, more disorderly, members of the college lived there!

When the German traveller, Zacharias von Uffenbach, visited Merton College in 1710, he criticised its 'several ugly old buildings' and, in the 1860s, the College considered sacrificing Mob Quad for a large new quadrangle. Butterfield's Grove Building (1864) was a compromise, setting a tall four storey Tudor style block beside the historic quad. The structure aroused fierce controversy, foreshadowing similar environmental battles in the 20th and 21st centuries, and Merton eventually had the top storey removed and the building re-faced in Box stone (1930, T. H. Hughes). Beyond the Grove Building, you come to a gate which provides access through a much reduced Merton Grove to Merton Street. This path is the successor of the route to the city wall 'in times of warr and distraction' which Walter de Merton agreed to maintain in 1266.

You are now directed southwards, but you can first enjoy a glimpse of the south front of Corpus Christi College Fellows' Building (1706–12, William Townesend). This is like a grand country house, three storeys high and eleven bays wide with a central pediment on Ionic pilasters. Until 1782, the college toilets were located behind the city wall at this point, but the area was then cleared to form a garden, and the old wall was lowered to provide Corpus with a view over the meadow. Further on, the city wall regains its full height and reaches a bastion which now incorporates a below-ground lecture room. The original Saxon ramparts would have continued west towards the South Gate, but Henry I allowed St Frideswide's Priory to expand southwards and re-align the defences in 1122. Later buildings have completely obscured this section of the city wall. Meanwhile, you are walking beside a high rubble stone wall which forms the eastern boundary of Christ Church Masters' Garden (1926). An iron gateway allows you a view of this delightful garden which consists of a central lawn surrounded by gravel paths and herbaceous borders. The setting is incomparable, from Meadow Buildings to your left past the Deanery and the Cathedral to the city wall and mature trees in front of Corpus Christi.

Merton Field, like the rest of Christ Church Meadow, was traditionally let for grazing but, by 1835, its unofficial use as 'a playground for all the Children in the town' had reduced its agricultural value. By 1898, Christ Church Cathedral School had taken over part of the field for cricket and was seeking improved measures to keep cattle off the pitch. School sport now reigns supreme on

27. Christ Church Masters' Garden and Cathedral

Merton Field and you will probably have been passed by many joggers along the way. The recreational use of Christ Church Meadow goes back centuries, and Walter de Merton was allowed to make a postern gate in the city wall in 1266 so that members of his new college could go 'walking into the fields.' By 1578, there was a perimeter walk around much of the meadow marked by a double row of trees, and Dean John Fell had the Broad Walk laid out in 1668–9, using stone from Wolsey's unfinished chapel on the north side of Tom Quad. Anthony Wood noted the planting of 72 elm trees on both sides of the new walk in 1670. The walk was initially known as the White Walk from the white stone, but the name was later corrupted to Wide and thus to Broad. From the first, and still of course today, the Broad Walk provided an outstanding view of Oxford's architecture. In the 19th century, it also became the focus for the annual Show Sunday promenade which marked the beginning of Commemoration Week. Citizens of all ranks, and their children, trooped along the Broad Walk, enjoying the spectacle as members of the University and their visitors paraded up and down in their finery. In 1863, while Henry Liddell was Dean of Christ Church, the Broad Walk elm avenue was extended westwards towards Christ Church stables, and his daughter, Alice, was among those called upon to plant the new trees. The 17th century elms were said to be falling like ninepins in 1912 and their replacements fell victim to Dutch elm disease in 1975. The loss of this avenue made Oxford's towers and spires newly visible from distant corners of the meadow and Christ Church decided to plant fewer trees in the Broad Walk so that some of these unexpected views would be preserved.

Turn right into the Broad Walk and head for Christ Church Meadow Buildings. Just before you reach them, an iron gate (1927, John Coleridge) ornamented with coats of arms, cardinals' hats and floral decoration will probably tempt you to have another look at the Masters' Garden. Built on the site of a 17th century block, Meadow Buildings (1862–6, T.N. Deane) provided 57 sets of rooms in what Pevsner described as a 'big, heavy Gothic Chinese Wall shutting off the meadow.' The building is of Box stone with Mansfield brick and Hornton stone dressings, but lacks much of the foliage carving that the architect envisaged. The south façade has a tower with very steep gables, and is otherwise of three storeys with attic dormers and tall chimney stacks. The Venetian style first floor balconies used to be adorned with sun blinds. Walking on past Meadow Buildings, you reach a roadway which leads off right towards St Aldate's. The square ashlar stone building you can see above the wall to the right is now Christ Church Senior Common Room, but it was built as an Anatomy School (1766–7, Henry Keene; rebuilt 1970). Carts brought the bodies of criminals and paupers from London for dissection and the gateway in St Aldate's became known as Skeleton Corner. On the other side of the roadway, Christ Church built a high stone wall in 1832 to keep out the stench of Trill Mill Stream which had become a virtual open sewer. You will notice that this wall was lowered and partly removed for the Christ Church Memorial Garden (1926–7) which we shall explore from St Aldate's later.

Until the 1870s, the perimeter walk around Christ Church Meadow kept to the roadway between Trill Mill Stream and the 19th century thatched stone barn which now forms part of the Christ Church visitor centre (2019, Purcell). This route lost its appeal when the stream became polluted and the growing popularity of rowing required something better than a 'narrow, damp, and unsavoury path' to the river. In 1872, Dean Liddell had the New Walk laid out in a direct line from the tower of Meadow Buildings to the river where college barges were now being moored. The walk was planted with an avenue of elm and lime trees which were replaced by black poplars in the 1920s; the latter are now giving way to limes. As you head down New Walk towards the river, you can enjoy the glorious tranquillity of the scene and perhaps the sight of longhorn cattle grazing, but it is worth considering here the road that never was, Christ Church Meadow Road. This was a saga so controversial in its day that a Cabinet containing many ex-Christ Church men allegedly placed the issue higher up the agenda than the Suez Canal crisis!

28. Longhorn cattle in Christ Church Meadow (*not shown on map*)

The City Engineer first hinted at a road across Christ Church Meadow as a 'possible extension from St Aldate's to Iffley Road' in 1935 and the Dean of Christ Church was aware of this plan by 1937. Lawrence Dale published *Christ Church Mall, a Diversion* in 1941, proposing a route close to the river. Thomas Sharp's proposed Merton Mall in 1948 was more radical, running from The Plain across Merton Field and the Broad Walk to emerge at a roundabout in St Aldate's south of the Memorial Garden. He argued that the choice lay between 'madder and more murderous congestion' in High Street or the sacrifice of 'quietness only' in Christ Church Meadow. Sharp's plan was at first dismissed, but it surfaced again after a public inquiry in 1953. Christ Church promised to oppose the scheme by every means, describing it as 'one of the greatest acts of vandalism that could be perpetrated.' Following Sir Frederick Armer's inquiry in 1961 which backed a route across the middle of the meadow as Oxford's inner relief road, Geoffrey Jellicoe produced a proposal for a sunken road in 1963. With landscaping and tree planting, he claimed that the illusion of an intact meadow could be maintained, but he had to admit that, with lighting, it would 'be an inferno at night.' This route was included in the City's 1964 Development Plan, but the inspector considering the plan rejected it, and a subsequent study came up with an alternative urban motorway proposal south of the river in 1968 which spared the meadow. In 1973, the City Council adopted *A Balanced Transport Policy* and all talk of urban motorways in Oxford ceased.

After you cross the Shire Lake ditch, you have the option to turn right on to a path which leads to the old route beside Trill Mill Stream. That is interesting for views of the river channel and modern

29. College barge, formerly moored at Dean's Ham (*not shown on map*)

development behind St Aldate's, but Dean Liddell's New Walk is certainly more beautiful. Keeping to the main walk brings you out at Dean's Ham where a wonderful array of college barges used to be moored from the 1850s until more practical boathouses replaced the last of them in the early 1960s. The barges and New Walk feature memorably in Max Beerbohm's novel *Zuleika Dobson* where Oxford undergraduates are driven to mass suicide by drowning through their passion for that *femme fatale*. The river at this point is often animated by practising rowers and passing pleasure craft; in winter, you should see some of Salter Bros. steamers moored here. Across the river, you can glimpse Grandpont House (c.1785), a three storey stuccoed house built on arches over a side stream of the Thames for William Elias Taunton, a successful lawyer who was Oxford's Town Clerk between 1795 and 1825. The east elevation facing the river has a tall Venetian window on the first floor set between two three-sided bays with tall sash windows. Alderman Thomas Randall (1804–87), an Oxford hatter, and the possible inspiration for Lewis Carroll's Mad Hatter, was a later resident of the house.

To the right of Grandpont House, Isis House (c.1850) is hidden in the trees and easily missed. Beyond a towpath bridge, the circular glazed stair tower of Hertford College's Graduate Centre (2000, Oxford Architects' Partnership) is a prominent feature. This building occupies the site of wharves used from the 1870s by boat builders, Salter Bros. For much of the 19th century, the Thames navigation lay along the river channel between these wharves and the warehouse opposite. Folly Bridge Lock was situated in this channel between 1821 and 1884, and the weather-boarded lock-keeper's house survived beside the towpath until 1999.

30. Grandpont House

The picturesque half-timbered and gabled building you can see on Folly Bridge island (1900, Stephen Salter) provided a boathouse and offices for Salter Bros., on the site of the former Boat House Tavern.

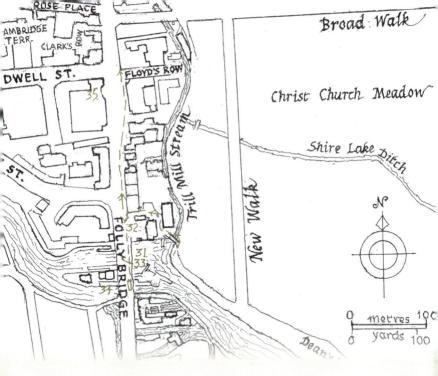

10 Folly Bridge to Speedwell Street

Looking towards Folly Bridge from this peaceful corner of Christ Church Meadow, you are essentially seeing the result of a major reshaping of the area in the 1820s when there was considerable traffic on both the Abingdon road and the river Thames. A new Folly Bridge (1825–7, Ebenezer Perry) replaced the decayed medieval and later bridge following an Act of Parliament in 1815. The bridge has three rusticated stone arches, and it was built of Headington stone; the very different parapets are of stone from the Forest of Dean, presumably transported by canal and river, because high quality local stone was not readily available.

There was commercial navigation on the Thames in Anglo-Saxon times, but use of the river below Oxford seems to have died out in the late medieval period. In 1603, an Act of Parliament appointed Commissioners to make the Thames navigable between Oxford and Burcot, near Dorchester, and the first barge reached the wharf at Folly Bridge on August 31st, 1635. Stone from the Oxford area could now be more easily transported to London, and coal and other supplies brought up to Oxford. Unusual river cargoes included collections for the new Ashmolean Museum in 1683 and lead statues for the Clarendon Building in 1712 which lay on the wharf for over two years, pending payment. The statues would have complemented the fine wharf house, similar to Vanbrugh House in St Michael's Street, which was erected beside the bridge in the early 18th century. That property was demolished in 1826 to make way for the new Folly Bridge, and replaced by the ashlar stone wharf house and warehouse (1827), now the Head of the River pub, on a more confined site.

It is now time to squeeze through the iron gate that leads out of Christ Church Meadow and explore the Folly Bridge area more closely. You cross Trill Mill Stream at its junction with the main river and walk up to St Aldate's between the Head of the River pub and Hertford College student accommodation, Warnock House (1995, Knowles & Son/ Nick Caldwell). The two blocks are known as 'Geoffrey' and 'Mary' after Sir Geoffrey Warnock (1923–95), philosopher and Principal of Hertford College between 1971 and 1988, and his wife, Mary (1924-2019), a philosopher who was made a life peer in 1985. The front block is neo-Georgian and of red brick with sash windows, loosely modelled on nos. 41–43 St Aldate's (c.1830), which incorporated the former Dolphin and Anchor pub. Eight-oared racing below Folly Bridge was first recorded in 1815, and the Eights had become an expected annual event by 1827–8. Early rowers had to share the river with decidedly unsympathetic bargees, but commercial traffic on the Thames declined quickly as the rail network grew and the Folly Bridge wharf was sold off in 1844. By 1851, Samuel Sidney noted that, 'Comedies, in the shape of sledging matches with the barges, are less frequent than formerly, and melodramatic fistic combats still less frequent.' A quieter river encouraged the growth of University rowing and the development of pleasure boating, and Oxford's watermen and boat builders soon adjusted to the new situation. Salter Bros., established in 1858, acquired the Folly Bridge wharf in 1870 and it lay at the heart of the firm's boat building and hiring business until the 1970s. Salter's also began operating passenger steamers on the Thames from Folly Bridge in 1886. Salter's Yard was threatened with demolition in the early 1970s, but it was successfully converted into the Head of the River pub in 1977. The name was inspired by the fact that the winning eight in the College Eights and Torpids races is celebrated as Head of the River.

A break in the open area outside the pub provides an opportunity to examine the preserved crane at close quarters and to notice the tall cast iron boundary railings which, in 1828, were said to be 'so insufficiently fastened as to shake upon being touched.' We also need to set the present scene into a deeper historical context since Folly Bridge is just one element in the ancient route which carried traffic across the Thames flood plain south of Oxford. This may have been in use by the end of the 7th century and there was evidently a substantial

31. Preserved crane from Salter's Yard, Head of the River pub

32. Iron railings, Head of the River pub

33. Friar Bacon's Study from a sketch by John Malchair, 1765

crossing here by c.900. Whether the original 'oxen ford' was south, west or indeed east of Oxford remains a matter of debate, but the southern approach certainly became pre-eminent in late Saxon times. Robert d'Oilly (d.1091 or 1092) improved it by building a series of stone bridges which created the Grandpont, or great bridge, with over 50 arches between St Aldate's and Cold Harbour in Abingdon Road.

Folly Bridge was known as South Bridge until the 17th century and New Gate, part of the town defences, was built on the bridge, probably in the late 13th century. This structure became known as Friar Bacon's Study because the Franciscan friar, Roger Bacon, was said to have used it for astronomical observations. The gate still had a drawbridge on either side in the late 16th century, but it no longer had any real defensive value and the City leased the building to Thomas Waltham, or Welcome, in 1602. He added a storey and converted it into a house which soon became known as Welcome's Folly, the folly from which Folly Bridge gets its name. The City established a waterworks south-east of Folly Bridge in 1694 which pumped river water into subscribers' homes, and the manager lived in the converted gate. Friar Bacon's Study was demolished as an obstruction to traffic in 1779, and the waterworks was moved to a new site north-west of Folly Bridge in 1826. Initially, it proved unable to supply any water at all when river levels were high, encouraging G.V. Cox to remark that the very name Folly Bridge was contagious!

Emerging in St Aldate's, you see opposite a single storey stuccoed toll house (1844), now a café. The cost of rebuilding Folly Bridge was met by tolls, collected initially at a toll gate further down Abingdon Road. A toll house was suddenly needed here in 1844 to intercept traffic to and from Oxford's first railway station which had just opened at the far end of what is now Western Road. Within six years the outstanding debt had been paid off, and the toll house was adapted to other uses. The listed building was retained in 1971 when Isis Street behind it was cleared and nearly became the site of a Churchill Hotel. The concrete columns for that unrealized scheme became another local folly until the Shire Lake Close development (1983–4) brought housing back to the area.

A short detour across Folly Bridge takes you past the site of Friar Bacon's Study and offers a splendid view downstream towards Iffley. West of the bridge, the main river channel turned sharply north-west towards today's Thames Street until the 1820s, and Robert Burton (1577–1640), Christ Church student and author of *The Anatomy of Melancholy*, apparently came down here regularly to enjoy watching bargemen curse and swear as they struggled to manoeuvre their vessels. When Folly Bridge was rebuilt, the old river channel was infilled, and a new channel, today's main stream, was cut through Ireland Mead to form a dock where barges could be loaded and unloaded. This left a narrow island south-west of the bridge used initially as a coal wharf but occupied by houses from the 1840s as commercial traffic on the Thames declined.

The most dramatic of these houses is no. 5 Folly Bridge (1849), formerly North

34. Caudwell's Castle, 5 Folly Bridge

Hinksey House. This red brick house ornamented with statues was built for Joseph Caudwell, a local accountant who clearly intended it as a folly to match the name of the bridge. The figure of Atlas, now without his globe, stands on the battlemented parapet overlooking the main road. Caudwell stationed cannons on his forecourt and the building was soon nicknamed Caudwell's Castle. It became a target for high-spirited undergraduates, but the fun ended in 1851 when Caudwell shot and injured one of the students who was trying to pull a cannon into the river. At his trial, Caudwell argued successfully that he had been acting in self-defence, but he subsequently left Oxford. Down the passageway beside no. 5, a later house (1875, George Shirley) was crenellated in 1974 to match Caudwell's folly. Opposite no. 5 Folly Bridge, Salter's three storey warehouse (1835–6, Thomas Greenshields) beside the former navigation channel was designed to be converted into a house should the need arise. It was built for boatbuilders, Carter, Sherratt and Hall who felt that 'the ornamental buildings is not essential or necessary for the business now carried on, yet the improvements in the immediate neighbourhood requires something to be done to perfect the approach to Oxford'.

Now re-cross Folly Bridge to reach Thames Street where prominent offices at nos. 58–60 St Aldate's (1990, Spiromega Partnership) were said to be 'in keeping with the traditional style of Oxford's architecture'. The block was originally known as Saxon Beck after the Shire Lake, the river channel which marked the original boundary between Oxfordshire and Berkshire. Denchworth Bow, one of the Grandpont arches, carried St Aldate's across this stream, which silted up following changes to the river in the 1820s and was finally filled in during 1884. Today's offices are on the site of a large National School (1813), built to take the boys of the University's Greycoat Charity School, founded in 1708, and many more besides. The venture was initially a great success, but the growth of parish schools reduced pupil numbers and the Greycoat School moved to new premises behind the University Press in Jericho in c.1829. The old school was used as a House of Observation during the 1832 cholera epidemic, but it was demolished in the 1840s. St Aldate's was then widened at this point, and Thames Street was formed, originally as a *cul de sac* leading to riverside yards and warehouses. In 1968, Thames Street was extended through St Ebbe's to provide a link with Westgate and Oxpens Road. South Oxford School (1910, W.H. Castle), now converted to flats, is the only survivor from old Thames Street. It is a two storey red brick building with large 'healthy' sash windows in the south-facing elevation and separate marked entrances for Boys and Girls at either end. Notice the terracotta panels above these entrances bearing the arms of the City and the date 1910. The school originally provided accommodation for 580 children in what was then a crowded part of Oxford, but numbers fell as the area became depopulated and it finally closed in 1981.

Looking north up St Aldate's from Thames Street to Speedwell Street, you may well wonder what became of all the historic sites and buildings in this ancient thoroughfare. Standing here a century ago, you would have seen a continuous frontage of two and three storey properties receding into the distance with Tom Tower just visible above the varied roofline. Over 1,300 people lived in St Aldate's parish in 1901, many of them living in these houses or in crowded courts and yards behind the street frontage. The bustling street was full of shops, pubs and businesses such as Basson & Co.'s City Saw Mills. The whole scene was the product of centuries of development, beginning in the late 11th century when people built houses on the east side of the causeway which provided some protection from flooding. House-building west of the causeway was under way by c.1225 after the land had silted up and been raised by dumping.

The low-lying part of St Aldate's outside the South Gate was known as Southbridge Street in c.1225, and later as Grandpont (1282) or Grampoole (1470). It was Bridge Street in 1750, but Fish Street, like the northern part of St Aldate's, by 1772; the modern name was in use by 1850. The decline of Oxford's population in the late 14th and 15th centuries left plots vacant in this area and there were still many gaps in the street frontage in 1578. By 1644, when a census established that 408 'strangers' were living in the parish during the Civil War, those gaps had been filled. Loggan, in 1675, also shows considerable backland development in St Aldate's, and that intensified in the late 18th and early 19th centuries as the city's population grew. Old drawings and photographs illustrate fine timber-framed 17th century houses on the east side of St Aldate's, but there were growing calls for the road to be widened, especially during the years that the railway station lay south of Folly Bridge. In 1925, as motor traffic increased and St Aldate's became part of the A34, the City Council agreed that the road south of Christ Church should be widened to 50 feet. This decision effectively condemned all the buildings fronting the east side of the road, but the task was only completed in 1967.

Many old properties fell victim to slum clearance. In 1919, the Rector of St Aldate's joined the Rector of St Ebbe's and other prominent signatories in a petition to the Medical Officer of Health, A. L. Ormerod, urging him to draw the City Council's attention to the unhealthiness of both parishes. Ormerod recommended tackling an area in St Ebbe's but, in 1923, the City chose to start with English Row on the west side of St Aldate's. The site included 61 houses with 242 occupants who had to be re-housed in new council houses at Cold Harbour in Abingdon Road. Clearance only began in 1929 but, following the Housing Act in 1930, the City identified another nine clearance areas in the parish during the 1930s. This large-scale destruction excited surprisingly little opposition. The Society for the Protection of Ancient Buildings worried about the east side of St Aldate's in 1919, but E.H. New, writing on behalf of the Oxford Architectural and Historical Society, reported that 'there is we think no building of real value though the general effect is picturesque.' The future historian, A. L. Rowse, who was an undergraduate in the early 1920s, described St Aldate's as 'the wretchedest poor quarter that there is in Oxford' with courts that were 'dismal shanties with roofs all askew and walls cracking; no drainage, no gardens, all the washing hung out on lines across the alleys. It was left to a later undergraduate, Michael Bunney, to see the potential of some of these courts in the early 1930s. He thought Shepperd's Row was 'a very pleasant row of late 17th century cottages' and Wyatt's Yard 'a row of very pleasing late 17th century cottages of coursed rubble two storeys and an attic in height.' At a time when major buildings like the Old Palace were still under threat, however, these humble rows and courts were doomed.

On the west side of St Aldate's, no. 61, the former Apollo pub (c.1866) is now the oldest surviving building between Thames Street and Speedwell Street, erected after the Paving Commissioners widened the road here in the late 1850s. Notice the ceramic plaque illustrating the artist George Morland which confirms that the Apollo was a Morland's of Abingdon pub. Next comes the very plain ashlar stone-fronted Crown Court building (1982) which incorporated the classical façade of the Morris Garages block (1932, Harry W. Smith). A sculpture of Lord Nuffield (1989, Martin Jennings) on the modern building recalls the link with the local motor industry. The retained portion of Morris Garages formed the showroom and offices of a vast building which included petrol pumps, repair facilities and Oxford's first multi-storey car park, where customers could leave their vehicles while shopping or going out for the evening. The sheer scale of the place, compared with the old showroom in Queen Street and Morris's garage in Longwall Street, reflected the huge increase in car ownership in just two decades. The building occupied the cleared English Row site and reflected how St Aldate's was being rapidly transformed into a commercial centre and traffic corridor. Excavations on the forecourt during the Crown Court development delved into the origins of the area, revealing an otherwise unknown river channel with a stone crossing which the archaeologist Brian Durham was tempted to identify as the original 'oxen ford'. Until the late 1960s, the junction with Speedwell Street lay further north, and F. J. Wigmore & Son's dairy was at nos. 77–8 St Aldate's, noted for its

35. Crown Court, former Morris Garages, and bas relief of Lord Nuffield, St Aldate's

cool tiled corner shop. Frank Wigmore had taken over a much older business in c 1887 and, ten years later, he was supplying most of his milk from Chilswell Farm above South Hinksey.

On the opposite side of St Aldate's, South Bridge Row (1979) provided welcome social housing, but the dreary brickwork rather than a stucco finish was much criticised at the time. The row filled a gap created when the former St Aldate's School (1866) and nearby properties had been demolished for one of the abortive Meadow road schemes. Further on, you reach Macmillan House and the entrance to St Aldate's Courtyard (1988, Perry Associates) before coming to the City Police Station (1938, City Estates Surveyor/H.F. Hurcombe). A.R. Woolley described the latter as 'a monument to the skinflint economies of the early nineteen-thirties', but the 'blankly classical' building of Bladon ashlar stone was a vast improvement on the old police station in Blue Boar Street. The detectives' department was on the first floor and, as the plaque on the frontage testifies, the building has achieved international fame through Colin Dexter's fictional character, Inspector Morse.

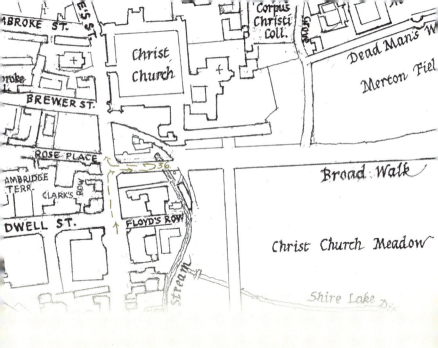

11 Speedwell Street to Christ Church

Speedwell Street and Floyd's Row opposite betray no sign of antiquity today. Speedwell Street is first recorded as Overhee Lane in 1190, when it would have led into the low-lying meadows west of St Aldate's. Later, it became a route to the Blackfriars and the friary mill, and was variously known as Butterwick Lane (14th–15th centuries), Mill Lane (15th–17th centuries), and Preachers' Lane (mid 17th century); the current name, perhaps recalling wild flowers in long-vanished meadows, was in use by 1850. Speedwell Street was extended through to St Ebbe's in the 1830s when Treadwell's market garden on the Blackfriars site was laid out for building. From 1948 onwards, Speedwell Street seemed likely to become the western continuation of Thomas Sharp's Merton Mall, and it was widened during the re-shaping of St Ebbe's roads in the late 1960s. As part of that process, Speedwell House (1972–4, Olins John Associates) was built as shops and offices on the site of nos. 79–81 St Aldate's. Excavations here traced development back to the 13th century, but the three storey building on the site had been largely rebuilt in the 19th century. Charles Raworth and Son, established as carriage builders in 1819, occupied nos. 79–80 for many years, and supplied the bodies for early Morris cars.

Across St Aldate's, Floyd's Row was one of several backland developments that began to occupy vacant space between the main street and the Trill Mill Stream during the 17th century. On the north side, there was a row of two storey cottages of rendered timber-framing with wide sash windows which were probably built in around 1800. The south side was more mixed, with small brick houses and several much older timber-framed properties behind no. 20 St Aldate's. Housing conditions here were undoubtedly poor, and one property became briefly notorious during the First World War as a brothel used by soldiers stationed in Oxford. Floyd's Row was subsequently cleared, but the old name was retained for a street of new civic buildings, the City Police Station, the former Labour Exchange (1936, Ministry of Works/ P. M. Stratton; converted to an emergency hostel 2020) and a coroner's court and mortuary (1939).

North of Speedwell Street, you at last begin to get a real sense of St Aldate's as an ancient street. Beyond the Tesco Express store, the importance of properties such as nos. 82–3, or Littlemore Hall, and the Old Palace had long been recognized and, in 1936, nos. 89–92 were also included in a published short-list of Oxford houses 'especially worthy of preservation.' These buildings had been very much at risk in the early 1920s when the City Council considered widening St Aldate's on both sides, and the roundabout proposed at the west end of Merton Mall in 1948 would have destroyed everything south of the Old Palace. In 1954, however, all the historic houses in this group were listed, and they make a vital contribution to the street scene. Nos. 82–3 St Aldate's are known as Littlemore Hall from an academic hall on the site during the 14th century. The present two storey rubble stone house was built in the 15th century, and remodelled in the early 17th century. There are two timber-framed gabled attic dormers over no. 82 and a large gable over no. 83 with a Welsh slate roof. Some of the stone mullioned and casement windows are modern replacements, but the mullioned windows on the first floor are 17th century originals.

Alice's Shop now occupies no. 83, which the artist Sir John Tenniel famously used as the model for the Sheep's Shop which Alice 'wanted to look all round' in Lewis Carroll's *Through the Looking Glass*. The next house, no. 84, has an 18th century four storey front of rendered timber framing with sash windows on the upper floors. As is so often the case, this plain façade masks a much older building which, in part, dates back to c.1600. Beyond Clark's Row, no. 85 is a late 18th century three storey house with a stuccoed front, perhaps masking an earlier building. The first floor bay window was added in 1877 and the Georgian-style shop front is modern. You next come to the Old Palace which has an east elevation of ashlar stone with a Dutch gable which scarcely prepares you for the spectacular timber-framed north elevation to Rose Place. The house was formerly known as Bishop King's Palace after Robert King, the first Bishop of Oxford (d.1557), but the building post-dates him and no bishop has ever lived here. The house was built in two sections, the smaller west range furthest from St Aldate's probably by the tanner, Edward Barkesdale (d.1596). The wealthy brewer, Thomas Smith, later acquired the property, and added the main house abutting St Aldate's (c.1622–8). The older part has two gables and the newer portion five large gables. The elevation is jettied, and the upper floors have pargetted decoration and oriel windows. Each oriel rests on three brackets carved with grotesques, and the middle one on the first floor bears the date 1628. The building was in poor condition by the end of the 19th century, but it was sympathetically restored (1919, F. F. Mullett) and again in 1952–3 when the east elevation was re-fronted.

Reaching Rose Place brings you to the site of Trill Mill Bow, the northernmost arch in the Grandpont, or great causeway. Until the 1920s, St Aldate's narrowed sharply at this point as the road approached the site of the South Gate in the city wall, and the street opposite the Old Palace was dominated by the Green Dragon pub (c.1796), a three storey building of stuccoed timber-framing with large sash windows. This had been built over Trill Mill Stream and occupied the site of Trill Mill Hall, an academic hall which flourished in the 14th century.

The City Council began to consider widening St Aldate's south of Christ Church in 1912 and, in 1919, it sponsored a competition for a housing scheme on the east side of the street between the Green Dragon site and Wyatt's Yard near Folly Bridge. Nothing came of this ambitious proposal, but the City and Christ Church demolished old properties between the College and Floyd's Row in 1924–5 to widen the street.

The City Council now owned the southern portion of the cleared site and initially intended to redevelop it on a commercial basis. Gilbert Gardner drew up a scheme for shops and flats in 1926, but newly-revealed views of Christ Church encouraged comparisons with Edinburgh, and local voices preferring a 'Princes Street solution' in St Aldate's were ultimately successful. In 1929, the City sold the land to the University which set the new rubble stone building for St Catherine's Society (1936, Sir Hubert Worthington) well back from the street. St Catherine's Society was the re-named Delegacy for Non-Collegiate Students and moved here from its Victorian premises in High Street next to the Examination Schools. After St Catherine's moved to new college buildings in Holywell in 1962, the all-graduate Linacre College (established 1962) occupied these premises. The growth of trees along the northern boundary had masked more distant views of Christ Church by the time the University's Faculty of Music took over the property in 1981 and a matching extension to Worthington's characteristic building was then added closer to St Aldate's. On weekday afternoons, you can visit the world-class Bate Collection of Musical Instruments, named after Philip Bate who gave his collection to the University in 1968.

Christ Church Memorial Garden quite fortuitously occupied the cleared site nearest the College. Christ Church had wanted to build at least 30 extra rooms as a useful memorial to college members and employees who had died in the Great War but, despite a £500 donation by the King of Siam, the appeal failed to raise enough money. The idea of using the fund for a memorial garden was first mooted as an alternative in 1924, and the design submitted by John Coleridge was put in place in 1926–7. The Memorial Garden is separated from St Aldate's by wrought iron screens between stone piers and you enter through one of the pedestrian gates beside the magnificent double gate (1927, R. M. Y. Gleadowe) which bears the College coat of arms. Inside this gate, notice a sword set in the stone paving and the nearby quotation from Bunyan's Pilgrim's Progress:

> 'My sword I give to him
> That shall succeed me in my pilgrimage.'

Thousands of visitors pass through the garden today, and pause to photograph the lovely herbaceous borders and the remarkable backdrop of buildings which includes Wolsey's Great Quad and Hall (c.1525–9), and the prominent Bell Tower (1876–8, Bodley & Garner). Their photographs inevitably incorporate the single storey college garage (1927, John Coleridge) which fits harmoniously into the scene with a rubble stone rear elevation and stone slate roof. Continuing through the garden, you come to a stone footbridge below which the Trill Mill Stream at last escapes into the daylight. Trill Mill probably lay to the south of this footbridge, and was first mentioned by name in the late 12th century when it was granted to St Frideswide's Priory. The name reflects the rushing of water through mill wheels, and a reduced flow perhaps led to the decline of Trill Mill and its total disappearance by the mid 17th century. It is now hard to imagine this little stream powering water mills or even to envisage the time when intrepid boaters such as the young T. E. Lawrence (Lawrence of Arabia) could go underground here and explore St Ebbe's from below. South of the pathway and beyond Trill Mill Stream, a delightful circular garden with a central fountain is set in front of a high red brick-faced wall. This wall, of rubble stone on the other side, was adapted in the 1920s from the one Christ Church had erected 100 years earlier to keep sewage smells at bay!

Retrace your steps to St Aldate's to admire the houses on the west side of the street between Rose Place and Brewer Street. North of Rose Place, no. 88 is a tall, ashlar stone house (c.1860) with two gables to the street and a two storey bay to the left of the central door.

36. Trill Mill Stream from stone footbridge, Christ Church Memorial Garden

The history of the property can be traced back to 1279, and it was originally an academic hall called Water Hall. The next house, no. 89, was a mid 18th century house with a stuccoed front and a two-columned Doric pedimented porch which retained elements of an earlier structure. After a lengthy planning dispute, it was replaced in 1985 by a new building of similar appearance which incorporated some historical fittings from the listed building. Excavations revealed a 9th century leather shoe and proved that there had been buildings on the site since the 13th century. No. 90 (c.1800) is a two storey stucco-fronted house with a hipped mansard slate roof. The double gates to the right form a circle with the archway above, and imitate the design of a humbler predecessor which probably led to livery stables. No. 91 may date back to the 17th century, but what you see is a three storey rough-cast timber-framed front of c.1782, complete with contemporary doorframe and sash windows, moulded cornice and parapet. Its early 17th century neighbour, no. 92, retains two gables, but the two storey roughcast timber-framed house was later altered with sash windows and a Welsh slate roof. The east elevation of no. 1 Brewer Street (1596) also had two gables until the 19th century, but this ashlar stone house was subsequently adapted and now has a north-facing front door.

Back on the east side of St Aldate's, a high stone wall brings you to Cutler's Gate – the one-time Skeleton Corner – which was set back when the road was widened in the mid 1920s. It is now a private entrance to Christ Church, but was the usual way into Christ Church Meadow before the Memorial Garden was created.

In medieval times, the lane was known as Schelving-Stole, perhaps from a ducking stool on the Trill Mill Stream. There were then several houses in the lane, but these vanished as the population of Oxford declined. A few houses also occupied the St Aldate's frontage between this lane and St Michael at the South Gate Church in the 13th century. The last two properties here were demolished in 1694 when Christ Church replaced them with a rubble stone wall between the south-west corner of the College and Cutler's Gate.

Looking along Brewer Street, you are very much aware of a retained section of the city wall, and you need to imagine these defences continuing across St Aldate's at the South Gate and on around St Frideswide's Priory. The burh or planned town of Oxford laid out in c.900 was built on the gravel terrace above the flood plain of the rivers Thames and Cherwell, and the rising ground here led to this part of St Aldate's being sometimes known as Tower Hill. The southern ramparts of the Saxon town were therefore built on an easily defended site and it has been argued that they incorporated an earlier settlement based around a minster on the site of Christ Church. The foundation of this religious house in c.700 is bound up with the story of St Frideswide (d.727) who is thought to have been a king's daughter who became abbess here. A charter of 1004 provides the first written evidence of this minster but archaeological excavations in the area have identified burials back to the 7th and 8th centuries. The minster was re-founded as a house of canons in 1049, and re-formed as an Augustinian priory in 1122. Henry I authorized the diversion of the city wall to enlarge the precinct, and the Romanesque church, now Christ Church Cathedral, and cloisters were built in stages between the 1150s and 1190s.

There must have been a South Gate in the Saxon ramparts from the beginning, and the adjacent church of St Michael at the South Gate (c.1122–1525) may have formed part of these defences as did St. Michael at the North Gate in Cornmarket. The medieval South Gate seems to have been a vaulted tunnel with flanking towers, and Anthony Wood described it as 'an ornament to that end of the towne, well-guarded on each side with a larg fortification, and adorned with battlements on the top and ... the armes of England and France quartered.' Thomas Wolsey's Cardinal College led to the destruction of St Michael at the South Gate Church in 1525, and part of the gate was presumably demolished at the same time; the rest fell down in 1617.

Pressing on past the St Aldate's frontage of Christ Church, you have a good view of the former Christ Church almshouses opposite. They are two storeys high with a gable at each end, and built of ashlar stone above the plinth; the two-light windows have arched lights and hoodmoulds above them. Notice that the lower doorway is some four feet above the pavement, reflecting changes to the level of the footway. Wolsey founded the almshouses in c.1525 as part of his Cardinal College project, but they were left unfinished at his fall in 1529. Henry VIII re-founded them in 1546 to provide homes for 24 almsmen with pensions of £6 a year. Draft statutes required inmates to 'make no outragioue noyse in your Alms howse', to 'goe only to honest places and for honest purposes', and 'at all tymes indeavour youre selves to be well occupied and at no tyme to be ydell (sic).' The almshouses were restored (1834, H. J. Underwood) when the north range was demolished, but the last inmates, Crimean War veterans, were removed in 1868. Christ Church sold the buildings to Pembroke College in 1888, and they became the Master's Lodgings in 1928.

Reaching Tom Gate, you have a tantalizing glimpse into Tom Quad with the Mercury fountain in the centre. In order to make room for this huge quad, Wolsey extinguished Frideswide Lane, which had previously defined the northern boundary of the Augustinian Priory. The lane began just north of the Tom Gate and ran eastwards to Oriel Street which then extended further south than it does today. Wolsey also suppressed Civil School Lane further north and acquired properties between the two lanes for demolition. These included Burnell's Inn which occupied the site of the synagogue of Oxford's Jewish community.

Characteristically, Wolsey did a deal with Balliol College, owners of the building, by which he promised lands and benefices, which he was never able to deliver, instead of money. Tom Quad was left unfinished at Wolsey's fall, by which time little progress had been made on the vast chapel envisaged for the north side. The quad was eventually completed in 1668, when the St Aldate's front of Christ Church acquired today's symmetrical appearance with a north-west tower to match the south-west one built in the 1520s.

From Tom Gate you have a splendid view towards Pembroke Square and St Aldate's Church. This was opened up by road widening in the mid 1830s which involved the demolition of the north range of Wolsey's almshouses and old houses east of the church. The church itself was also considerably altered and extended during the 19th century, with additions to both aisles and a rebuilt tower and spire (1862 and 1873–4, J. T. Christopher). Beyond the church, no. 94 St Aldate's (1899, E. G. Cobb.) is a three storey white brick building which replaced a picturesque group of old houses on the corner of Pembroke Street. Margaret Woods, a former Oxford resident, wrote to the *Daily Chronicle* in 1898 criticizing plans to build this 'workhouse-like building'. She argued that 'The architectural beauty of Oxford is a matter of public interest as much as the beauty of a Rafael or a Titian.'

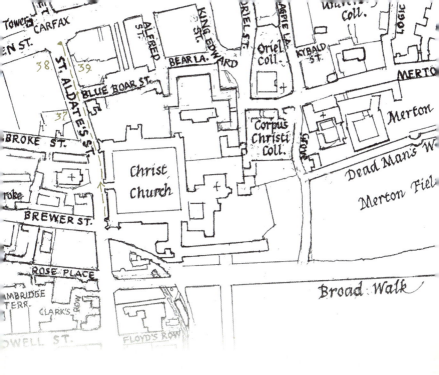

12 Pembroke Street to Town Hall

The northern part of St Aldate's was known as the Jewry or Great Jewry by c.1210 because many Jews lived in the area. It was convenient for business and close to the Castle if they needed to call for royal protection; from c.1228, their synagogue was also nearby, opposite the end of Pembroke Street. Jews had settled in Oxford by 1141 when Matilda and Stephen, the rival claimants to the throne, both demanded money from them. Local Jews such as David of Oxford, his wife, Licoricia, and Jacob of Oxford, who sold one of his properties to Walter of Merton, became extremely wealthy and they built substantial houses.

One such house on part of the Town Hall site was seized by Henry III in 1229 and sold on to the town as a guildhall. David of Oxford's house to the south was similarly confiscated in 1244, and ownership transferred to the Domus Conversorum (House of Converted Jews) in London. The City acquired the building in 1541 and it became the lower guildhall, surviving until a new Town Hall was erected in 1751. The Jewish community in medieval Oxford may never have exceeded 200 people, and its situation became less tenable when the nearby St Frideswide's Priory began to attract pilgrims to the saint's new shrine after 1180. In 1221, the

Blackfriars chose to begin their mission in the heart of the Jewry with a view to converting Jews 'by their exemplary carriage and gifts of preaching.' As a result of persecution, perhaps only about nine Jewish households remained in Oxford when Edward I finally expelled all Jews from England in 1290.

St Aldate's, from Carfax to Pembroke Street, was part of the street market place, and fish was sold here from the earliest times. By 1342, it was sometimes known as Fish Street, and that name was abandoned only gradually after 1774 when fishmongers were moved into the new Covered Market. The guildhall and the street outside also became the site of the annual St Frideswide's Fair after 1549 when Edward VI granted it to the City. This ancient fair had been granted to St Frideswide's Priory at its foundation in 1122 and was held in the priory precincts. It lasted for seven or eight days during which the canons benefited from a host of tolls and other profits. St Frideswide's Fair seems to have become an important cloth fair in the later medieval period, but the City's hopes of enjoying a good annual income from it were never realized. By 1663, it was 'hardly acknowledged to be a fair', but it lingered on into the 19th century when the historian J. R. Green recalled 'the cakestall which adorns St Aldate's' as the last relic.

Heading north behind 21st century bus shelters, you can't fail to notice the high rubble stone boundary wall on your right. Christ Church built this wall between the new north-west tower and the Bull Inn in 1668, adding some ground to the street in an early example of road widening. The Bull was a timber-framed building, first licensed as the Black Bull in 1646. It gave way (c.1830) to today's square, ashlar stone house which had an upstairs bay window added in 1886. Mathews Comfort & Co. Ltd. occupy the former Unicorn Inn, a 17th century timber-framed and stuccoed building with two gables facing St Aldate's and one in Blue Boar Street. Sash windows were added in the 18th and 19th centuries. A real tennis court existed behind the Unicorn by 1635 and, in c.1670, Thomas Burnham built 'a fair and stately Rackett Court ... covered over head which it was not before'. Tennis was played here until c.1835, and the building was used as a temporary theatre during university vacations with public access through the Bull; in August 1810, for example, Mr Russell's players were performing 'The Busy Body' and 'The Lying Varlet' there. Having ceased to be an alehouse, the Unicorn was for many years a University lodging house, one famous occupant being the poet, Hilaire Belloc.

On the other side of St Aldate's, nos. 95–7 (c.1871) replaced three old properties on the corner of Pembroke Street destroyed by fire on 29th June 1870. Two people died in the fire, and indignation about the delay in tackling the blaze led to the formation of the Oxford

37. Detail of carved frieze on the General Post Office, St Aldate's

Volunteer Fire Brigade in 1871. The present buildings are of white brick with stone dressings and three storeys high with attics. Further along, no. 98 takes us back to the late 18th century and has a three storey stuccoed timber-framed front with sash windows, a moulded cornice and parapet. Between 1876 and 1888, and ever since 1908, the Frewen Club has occupied upstairs rooms here; the landlord originally warned members that there was to be 'no spitting out of the window into the street.' Officers of the 2nd Corps, Oxford Rifle Volunteers founded the club in 1869 but it soon evolved into an Oxford gentlemen's club. It was based for a time in Frewin Court in Cornmarket, and the club's name probably reflects an alternative Victorian spelling. Nos. 99–100 St Aldate's are a pair of early 19th century houses, four storeys high and, unusually, of black brick with wide three-light sash windows and ashlar stone lintels. J. Venables & Son, gun makers (established 1790) occupied no. 99 for many years and the firm was still organising clay pigeon shoots around the county in the late 1960s. Almost dwarfed by the neighbouring Post Office building, the Old Tom pub at no. 101 has an early 19th century three storey stuccoed timber-framed front with a single sash window on each upper floor.

The General Post Office (1880, E.G. Rivers) is a grandiose Gothic building of ashlar stone, three storeys high with a tower. It reflects the self-confidence and the importance of the Victorian Post Office and the growth in business stimulated by the Penny Post, the railways and the telegraph; in 1842, two arches below the Town Hall had sufficed as the city's post office. Unfortunately, this new building replaced the historic Ducklington's Inn, erected in c.1300 by John of Ducklington (d. c.1336) on the site of one of many Jewish properties in this area. The original cellars of that building were recorded during the demolition of a fine three storey house that had for many years been the residence of Oxford surgeons. Beyond the Post Office, no. 107 St Aldate's has a 19th century three storey front with sash windows above the walk-in

38. Mr Therm on balcony of former gas company showroom, 117–19 St Aldate's

shop front. The photographer Charles Gillman occupied these premises between 1882 and 1910, and Oxford Photocrafts, architectural and commercial photographers, were later based here behind Alfred Savage's stationery shop. The St Aldate's Tavern at no. 108 (1897, H.W. Moore) has an exuberant three storey red brick front with sash windows and terracotta decoration, and it is a little reminiscent of the contemporary Royal Blenheim in St Ebbe's Street. The pub was known as the Bulldog from c.1965, after the nickname for the University officials who used to look out for erring undergraduates, but it was previously known – from 1716 – as the New Inn. It was a coaching inn until 1783 and New Inn Yard remains a central transport hub to this day, providing taxis where once there were horse-drawn cabs.

Some old stabling survives behind the pub in New Inn Yard but, further down, the picturesque 19th century premises of Taylor & Co.'s omnibus office gave way to car parking in 1969. The yard is in fact the stub of a lost street, Kepeharm's Lane, named after the member of the Oxford family who laid it out in c.1220. It is unclear whether the lane continued west into the modern St Ebbe's Street, north into Queen Street or perhaps into both; by 1606, it had been closed. Excavations on the Marks & Spencer site in the 1970s identified a house on the south side of the lane which was occupied by Thomas de Hensey in 1325/6, and later became an academic hall, Hinxey Hall, until 1536.

North of the New Inn, the west side of St Aldate's retained real individuality until the 1930s with three and four storey brick, stone and stuccoed fronts dating from the 18th and 19th centuries. The Society for the Protection of Ancient Buildings sent two artists, Hanslip Fletcher and Marisco Pearce, to record disappearing Oxford in September 1931. Pearce reported back to the Secretary: 'We found them destroying buildings opposite the Town Hall of some interest and made some drawings.' Nos. 114–16 were then being cleared for a new branch of Barclays Bank (1932) which set a pattern of tall, neo-Classical office buildings for the rest of the street. Nos. 117–19 (1939, G.T. Gardner) was built for the Oxford and District Gas Company, and included a demonstration kitchen as well as a large showroom; Mr Therm was already well-established as a promotional figure for the gas industry, and he still features on the first floor iron balconies. This building occupied the site of two former inns, the Red Lion and the Fleur de Luce; the latter had flourished in the 14th century as Battes Inn, and retained wine cellars of that date.

Back on the east side of St Aldate's, Blue Boar Street was formed in 1553 as a new northern boundary for Christ Church. It was sometimes known as Tresham's Lane, from William Tresham, Sub-Dean of Christ Church at the time, or as New Lane, but the name Blue Boar Lane was in use by the mid 17th century, recalling the major inn north of the Unicorn built in c.1550. When offered for sale in 1814, the recently re-fronted Blue Boar contained 17 good bed-chambers and boasted a

39. Beaver on lead rainwater pipe, Oxford Town Hall

40. City Mace Bearer (*not shown on map*)

new club room accommodating over 200 people; until 1866 an archway extended the building over the western end of Blue Boar Lane. The City purchased the property in 1864, and it was demolished in 1893 to make way for the present Town Hall (1893–7, H.T. Hare). Hare chose a 'mixed Renaissance' style for this large and showy building and his design was selected in an architectural competition that attracted 137 entries. The façade, with external sculpture by William Aumonier, is symmetrical, except for the south turret, and it has a crowning spirelet above the central doorway.

The Town Hall consciously expressed the new civic pride of a corporation which had, in 1889, achieved almost complete independence from the University in the government of the City. It proved to be an expensive gesture as the original estimate of £50,000 escalated to a final cost of £94,116, but Alderman Robert Buckell, the Liberal Chairman of the Municipal Buildings Committee, was supported by his Conservative rival, Alderman Walter Gray, through many a stormy debate and, as Mayor, he saw the project through to an official opening by the Prince of Wales, later Edward VII, on May 12th, 1897. The new building provided courts and a police station along Blue Boar Street, and a City Library tucked around the Blue Boar Street corner, approached by steps. Notice the Francis Bacon quotation above the door: 'Studies serve for delight, for ornament, and for ability.' The City Library moved to the Westgate Centre in 1973, and the Museum of Oxford opened in the old library in 1975. The main entrance in St Aldate's led to ground floor offices and, by means of an imposing staircase, to the richly decorated Main Hall, the Council Chamber, the Assembly Room and the Mayor's Parlour. You can experience some of this grandeur by attending events in the Town Hall or by going on a guided tour which will reveal memorable details such as the carved heads of Buckell, Gray and other members of the original building committee outside the Council Chamber. You can also explore the wider history of the city and its communities at the Museum of Oxford, redeveloped and extended in 2020.

Hare's building replaced a smaller, classical Town Hall (1751–2, Isaac Ware), and buildings in the Town Hall Yard which included Nixon's School (1658) and a large Corn Exchange (1861, S.L. Seckham). The ornamental stone doorway to Nixon's School was dismantled and re-erected in the garden of no. 92 Woodstock Road, then the home of Alderman Thomas Lucas. The new Town Hall did, however, retain the adjoining Oxford Trustee Savings Bank premises in St Aldate's (1867, Charles Buckeridge) which became the Town Clerk's offices. This fine Gothic building incorporated the probably 15th century vaulted cellar of Knap Hall, a medieval house north of the upper guildhall. Knap Hall was the Falcon Inn by the 15th century, and the Castle Inn by the 17th century, and this cellar once formed part of a web of inter-connecting wine-cellars, some of them beneath the streets. Buckeridge's building was lost to the Carfax improvement scheme in 1931, but the cellar was again preserved, and it now houses items from Oxford's impressive collection of civic plate which you can see during guided tours of the Town Hall. It is something of a culture shock to emerge from this quiet cellar into the bustle of 21st century Carfax, but where better to end a heritage walk than at the crossroads which has witnessed so much of Oxford's history.

Notes and Further Reading

Louise Allen, 375 Years of Celebration, *University of Oxford Botanic Garden and Harcourt Arboretum News* 24 (Summer 1996)

Nicholas Amherst, *Strephon's Revenge: a Satire on the Oxford Toasts* (1718)

P.W.S. Andrews and Elizabeth Brunner, *The Life of Lord Nuffield* (1959)

Annual Reports of the Medical Officer of Health for the City of Oxford

Norma Aubertin-Potter, *Oxford Coffee-Houses, 1651-1800* (1987)

William Bayzand, Coaching in and out of Oxford from 1820 to 1840, In, Collectanea vol. 4, *Oxford Historical Society* 47 (1905)

Cuthbert Bede, *The Adventures of Verdant Green* (1853)

Max Beerbohm, *Zuleika Dobson, or an Oxford Love Story* (1911)

P.G. Beresford, *St Ebbe's 1955-85* (1987)

E.G.W. Bill, *Christ Church Meadow* (1965)

John Blair, St Frideswide's Monastery: Problems and Possibilities, *Oxoniensia* 53 (1988)

John Blair, St Frideswide Reconsidered, *Oxoniensia* 52 (1987)

Philip Bliss, ed., *Hearnianae Reliquiae: the Remains of Thomas Hearne MA...*, vol. 1 (1857)

Bodleian Library, *University College: the First 750 Years* (1997)

A.J. Bott and J.R.L. Highfield, The Sculpture Over the Gatehouse at Merton College, Oxford, 1464-5, *Oxoniensia* 58 (1993)

Alan Bott, *Merton College: a Longer History of the Buildings and Furnishings* (2015)

Angela Boyle, Excavations in Christ Church Cathedral Graveyard, Oxford, *Oxoniensia* 66 (2001)

L.F. Bradburn, *The Old Bank, Oxford* (1977)

M.G. Brock and M.C. Curthoys, *History of the University of Oxford, vol. 7: the Nineteenth Century* (2000)

G.C. Brodrick, Memorials of Merton College, *Oxford Historical Society* 4 (1885)

M.J.H. Bunney & C.M. Pearce, *An Oxford Survey* (1935)

Carfax, pseud., *Christ Church Mall, a Diversion* (1941)

Andrew Clark, ed., The Life and Times of Anthony Wood, vol. 1, *Oxford Historical Society* 19 (1891)

Andrew Clark, ed., Survey of the Antiquities of the City of Oxford, by Anthony Wood, vol. 1, *Oxford Historical Society* 15 (1889)

Andrew Clark, ed., Survey of the Antiquities of the City of Oxford, by Anthony Wood, vol. 2, *Oxford Historical Society* 17 (1890)

G.V. Cox, *Recollections of Oxford* (1868)

Alan Crossley, ed., *Victoria History of the County of Oxford, vol. 4: the City of Oxford* (1979)

Judith Curthoys, *The Cardinal's College: Christ Church, Chapter and Verse* (2012)

Judith Curthoys, 'To Perfect the College...', the Christ Church Almsmen, 1546-1888, *Oxoniensia* 60 (1995)

Robin Darwall-Smith, *A History of University College, Oxford* (2008)

Robin Darwall-Smith, The Medieval Buildings of University College, *Oxoniensia* 70 (2005)

Mark Davies, *King of All Balloons: The Adventurous Life of James Sadler* (2015)

Mark Davies, Soaring into History, *Oxfordshire Limited Edition* (January 2016)

Anne Dodd, *Oxford Before the University* (2003)

Tony Dodd and Julian Munby, The Fate of the Trill Mill, *Oxoniensia* 70 (2006)

Brian Durham, The Thames Crossing at Oxford: Archaeological Studies, 1979-82, *Oxoniensia* 49 (1984)

Julia Dry, *Merton Walks, or the Oxford Beauties, a Poem* (1717)

Charles Fenby, *The Other Oxford* (1970)

Malcolm Graham, *On Foot in Oxford, no. 4: Folly Bridge and South Oxford* (1975)

Malcolm Graham, *Oxford Heritage Walk 4: From Paradise Street to Sheepwash* (2016)

Malcolm Graham, Oxford in the 1850s: Reminiscences of Henry Taunt, *Top Oxon* 18 (1972)

Malcolm Graham, *Oxford in the Great War* (2014)

Malcolm Graham, *Oxfordshire at War* (1994)

J.R. Green, *Oxford Studies* (1901)

R.T. Gunther, *A Guide to the Oxford Botanic Garden* (1914)

R.T. Gunther, *Oxford Gardens* (1912)

Claire Halpin, Late Saxon Evidence and Excavation of Hinxey Hall, Queen Street, Oxford, *Oxoniensia* 48 (1983)

S A Harris, *Oxford Botanic Garden and*

Arboretum: A Brief History (2017)
T.G. Hassall, Excavations at Oxford, 1970, Oxoniensia 36 (1971)
Trevor Hayward, Rocking Oxford (2009) Hertford College Magazine
Christopher Hibbert, The Encyclopaedia of Oxford (1988)
J.R.L. Highfield, The Early Colleges, In, J.I. Catto, ed., The History of the University of Oxford, vol. 1: the Early Oxford Schools (1984)
M.G. Hobson, Oxford Council Acts, 1701-1752 (1954)
R.S. Hoggar, Map of Oxford (1850)
Peter Howell, Oxford Architecture, 1800-1914, In, M.G. Brock and M.C. Curthoys, eds., History of the University of Oxford, vol. 7: 19th Century Oxford, Part 2 (2000)
Thomas Hughes, Tom Brown at Oxford (1861)
D.O. Hunter-Blair, In Victorian Days and Other Papers (1939)
Herbert Hurst, Oxford Topography: an Essay, Oxford Historical Society 39 (1899)
Herbert Hurst, Two Medieval Cellars in Oxford, Archaeologia Oxoniensis (1895)
Herbert Hurst, Visit to Cellars, Oxford Architectural & Historical Society Proceedings 6 (1894)
Edward Impey, The Rhodes Building at Oriel, 1904-2011: Dynamite or Designate? Oxoniensia 76 (2011)
P.D. John, Politics and Corruption: Oxford and the General Election of 1880, Oxoniensia 55 (1990)
Kelly's Directory of Oxford, Abingdon, Woodstock and Neighbourhood
Anthony Kemp, The Fortification of Oxford During the Civil War, Oxoniensia 42 (1977)
Frederick King, Reminiscences of Oxford During the Past 70 Years, Oxford Architectural and Historical Society Proceedings 6 (1894)
R.T. Lattey, A Contemporary Map of the Defences of Oxford, Oxoniensia 1 (1936)
Fiona MacCarthy, William Morris (1994)
Arthur MacGregor, The Ashmolean Museum: a Brief History of the Institution and its Collections (2001)
P.S. Manix, Beneath Our Feet: Oxford's Medieval Jewish Cemetery (2014)
P.J. Marriott, Oxford Pubs Past & Present (1978)
P.J. Marriott, The Young Lawrence of Arabia, 1888-1910 (1977)
G.H. Martin and J.R.L. Highfield, A History of Merton College (1997)
Joanna Matthews, Four Garden Ornaments in the Oxford Botanic Garden, Garden History, vol. 33, no.2 (2005)

Joanna Matthews, The Warwick Vase, University of Oxford Botanic Garden News 48 (Summer 2002)
Richard Mayou and Joanna Matthews, The Buildings of the Botanic Garden, University of Oxford Botanic Garden News 73 (Spring 2010)
Henry Minn, High Street South (Bodleian Library MS. Top. Oxon. d.498)
Henry Minn, St. Aldate's (Bodleian Library MS. Top. Oxon. d.503)
Henry Minn, South-East Ward (Bodleian Library MS. Top. Oxon. d.491)
Henry Minn, South-West Ward (Bodleian Library MS. Top. Oxon. d.492)
R.J. Morris, The Friars and Paradise: an Essay in the Building History of Oxford, 1801-1861, Oxoniensia 36 (1971)
Julian Munby, 126 High Street: the Archaeology and History of an Oxford House, Oxoniensia 40 (1975)
Julian Munby, J.C. Buckler, Tackley's Inn, and Three Medieval Houses in Oxford, Oxoniensia 43 (1978)
Julian Munby, Zacharias's: a 14th Century Oxford New Inn and the Origins of the Medieval Urban Inn, Oxoniensia 57 (1992)
Wendy Norbury, Oxford Town Hall: Planning, Building and Financing the Oxford Town Hall, Oxoniensia 65 (2000)
Revd Octavius Ogle, The Oxford Market, in Montagu Burrows, ed., Collectanea, vol. 1, Oxford Historical Society 16 (1890)
Philip Opher, Pocket Guide to Twentieth Century Oxford Architecture (1995)
Philip Opher and Olga Samuels, Gardens and Meadows, rev ed (1994)
Oxford Architectural and Historical Society, Old Houses in Oxford (1912)
Oxford City Council, Council Reports
Oxford City Council, Planning Applications
Oxford City Council, The Former Toll-house, Folly Bridge (1981)
Oxford Preservation Trust, Annual Reports
William Page, ed., Victoria History of the County of Oxford, vol. 2 (1907)
Harry Paintin, Articles on Oxford and District (c.1930)
W.A. Pantin, Domestic Architecture in Oxford, Antiquaries Journal 27 (1947)
Robert Peberdy, Navigation on the river Thames between London and Oxford in the late Middle Ages, Oxoniensia 61 (1996)
W.T. Pike, Views & Reviews Special Edition Oxford (1897)
Daniel Poore et al, Excavations at No. 4A

Merton Street, Merton College, Oxford, *Oxoniensia* 71 (2006)
W.H. & W.J.C. Quarrell, eds., *Oxford in 1710, from the Travels of Zacharias Conrad von Uffenbach* (1928)
A Report...into the State of the Sewerage, Drainage and Water Supply of the University and City of Oxford (1851)
E.S. Rohde, *Oxford's College Gardens* (1932)
Cecil Roth, *The Jews of Medieval Oxford*, Oxford Historical Society New Series 9 (1951)
E.C. Rouse, Some 16th and 17th Century Domestic Paintings in Oxford, *Oxoniensia* 37 (1972)
A.L. Rowse, *A Cornishman at Oxford* (1965)
Royal Commission on Historical Monuments England, *An Inventory of the Historical Monuments in the City of Oxford* (1939)
H.E. Salter, A Cartulary of the Hospital of St John the Baptist, vol. 1, Oxford Historical Society 66 (1914)
H.E. Salter, Cartulary of Oseney Abbey, vol.1, Oxford Historical Society 89 (1929)
H.E. Salter, Medieval Oxford, Oxford Historical Society 100 (1936)
H.E. Salter, *Oxford City Properties* (1926)
H.E. Salter, Survey of Oxford, vol. 1, Oxford Historical Society New Series 14 (1960)
H.E. Salter, Surveys and Tokens, Oxford Historical Society 75 (1920)
H.E. Salter, The Oxford Deeds of Balliol College, Oxford Historical Society 64 (1913)
H.E. Salter and M.D. Lobel, eds., *Victoria History of the County of Oxford: Volume 3, the University of Oxford* (1954)
C.L. Shadwell and H.E. Salter, *Oriel College Records* (1926)
Thomas Sharp, *Oxford Replanned* (1948)
Claire Sherriff, *The Oxford College Barges: their History and Architecture* (2003)
Jennifer Sherwood and Nikolaus Pevsner, *Oxfordshire* (1974)
W.E. Sherwood, *Oxford Rowing* (1900)
W.E. Sherwood, *Oxford Yesterday* (1927)
Samuel Sidney, *Rides on Railways* (1851)
David Sturdy, Houses of the Oxford Region, *Oxoniensia* 26/27 (1961/2)
David Sturdy, *Twelve Oxford Gardens* (1974)

Victor Sugden, *An Oxford Diary* (2009)
Ann Spokes Symonds and Nigel Morgan, *The Origins of Oxford Street Names* (2010)
F.S. Thacker, *The Thames Highway, Vol. 2 Locks and Weirs* (1920)
Chris Thorogood and Simon Hiscock, *Oxford Botanic Garden: A Guide* (2019)
Margaret Toynbee and Peter Young, *Strangers in Oxford* (1973)
Geoffrey Tyack, *Oxford: an Architectural Guide* (1998)
Geoffrey Tyack, *Stanford House, 64-70 High Street, Oxford* (2013)
University College Record
University of Oxford, *Botanic Garden and Harcourt Arboretum* (c. 2010),
W.M. Wade, *Walks in Oxford*, 2nd edn (1818)
John Walker, *Oxoniana*, (1809)
Timothy Walker, A Few Words…, *University of Oxford Botanic Garden & Harcourt Arboretum News* (86), Spring 2014
E.J. Warr, *The Oxford Plaque Guide* (2011)
S.R. Wigram, The Cartulary of the Monastery of St Frideswide at Oxford, vol. 1, Oxford Historical Society 28 (1895)
Anthony Wood, *The Ancient and Present State of the City of Oxford…with Additions by the Revd Sir J. Peshall* (1773)
A.R. Woolley, *The Clarendon Guide to Oxford* (1963)

https://en.wikipedia.org/
https://viewfinder.historicengland.org.uk/
https://www.heritagegateway.org.uk/
http://www.hertford.ox.ac.uk/accommodation/college-properties/
https://www.historicengland.org.uk/
https://historicengland.org.uk/images-books/archive/
https://www.merton.ox.ac.uk/about/history-merton
https://www.oxford.gov.uk/
https://www.oxforddnb.com/
http://www.oxfordhistory.org.uk/
http://www.oxfordshireblueplaques.org.uk/
http://www.thisisoxfordshire.co.uk/archive
https://www.univ.ox.ac.uk/about/college-buildings/